Implementing the Common Core State Standards through Mathematical Problem Solving

High School

Theresa J. Gurl
Alice F. Artzt
Alan Sultan
Queens College of the City University of New York

Frances R. Curcio, Series Editor
Queens College of the City University of New York

NCTM®

NATIONAL COUNCIL OF
TEACHERS OF MATHEMATICS

Copyright © 2012 by
The National Council of Teachers of Mathematics, Inc.
1906 Association Drive, Reston, VA 20191-1502
(703) 620-9840; (800) 235-7566; www.nctm.org
All rights reserved

ISBN: 978-0-87353-710-0

The Cataloging-in-Publication Data is on file
with the Library of Congress.

The National Council of Teachers of Mathematics is a public voice of mathematics education, supporting teachers to ensure equitable mathematics learning of thehighest quality for all students through vision, leadership, professional development, and research.

Printed in the United States of America

Contents

Series Editor's Foreword

The purpose of *Implementing the Common Core State Standards through Mathematical Problem Solving: High School*, as well as the other books in the series (those for K–grade 2, grades 3–5, and grades 6–8), is to (1) provide examples of how instruction that focuses on developing mathematical problem-solving skills supports the Common Core State Standards (CCSS), (2) help teachers interpret the standards in ways that are useful for practice, and (3) provide examples of rich mathematical tasks and ways of implementing them in the classroom that have specific links to multiple standards. The books in this series are not meant to be comprehensive collections of mathematics problems for the entire school curriculum; instead, they contain rich problems and tasks of selected topics designed to develop several mathematics concepts and presented in ways that illustrate the connections and interrelatedness between CCSS and mathematical problem solving.

The Common Core State Standards for Mathematics

In June 2010, responding to the declining achievement of U.S. schoolchildren in reading and mathematics both nationally and when compared internationally, the National Governors Association and the Council for Chief State School Officers issued the *Common Core State Standards* (http://www.corestandards.org). The CCSS program is an attempt at providing a unified, national effort to strengthen the ability of future citizens to be globally competitive, while preparing them for college and career readiness. The standards and practices across the grades are expectations for improving the teaching and learning of mathematics. Toward this concerted effort, a large majority of the states, along with the Washington, D.C., school system, have adopted the CCSS.

Similar to the *Principles and Standards for School Mathematics* (NCTM 2000), the essential content in the Common Core State Standards for Mathematics (CCSSM) is included in various degrees of specificity: Number and Quantity, Algebra, Functions, Modeling, Geometry, and Statistics and Probability, with modeling expected to be integrated throughout the other content areas. An overview of the CCSSM high school and middle school standards for mathematics is included in the Appendix.

For each content area, the eight Standards for Mathematical Practice, which may be considered as fundamental elements of mathematical problem solving, are listed:

CCSS Standards for Mathematical Practice

MP.1 Make sense of problems and persevere in solving them.

MP.2 Reason abstractly and quantitatively.

MP.3 Construct viable arguments and critique the reasoning of others.

MP.4 Model with mathematics.

MP.5 Use appropriate tools strategically.

MP.6 Attend to precision.

MP.7 Look for and make use of structure.

MP.8 Look for and express regularity in repeated reasoning. (CCSSI 2010)

These practices are highlighted throughout the problem-solving tasks and activities contained in each of the books in this series.

Mathematical Problem Solving

Although problem solving has always been a goal of mathematics instruction, Pólya's helpful guide, *How to Solve It* (1957), had been in print for several decades before the publication of *An Agenda for Action* in 1980, in which the National Council of Teachers of Mathematics (NCTM) asserted the importance of mathematical problem solving in the school curriculum. That is, *"the mathematics curriculum should be organized around problem solving"* (NCTM 1980, p. 2, original in italics).

But what is mathematical problem solving? Throughout the years, although not research-based, instruction in developing mathematical problem-solving skills has relied on Pólya's (1957) four-step approach: understanding the problem, developing a plan, carrying out the plan, and looking back to determine whether the solution makes sense.

At the heart of the problem-solving process is determining what a problem consists of for learners of mathematics. Different from a familiar exercise or example for which learners have a prescribed approach for obtaining a solution, a "problem" is usually non-routine and nontraditional, and the learner needs to bring strategies, tools, and insights to bear in order to solve it (Henderson and Pingry 1953). In the late 1980s, textbooks and supplemental resource materials highlighted various problem-solving strategies to assist learners in approaching and solving problems. Such strategies as guessing and checking, using a drawing, making a table or an organized list, finding a pattern, using logical reasoning, solving a simpler problem, and working backward (O'Daffer 1988) became staples of mathematics instruction.

Much of the research on mathematical problem solving was conducted in the mid-1970s through the late 1980s (Schoenfeld 2007). The intent was not to focus on solving a given problem but rather on examining how to help learners to develop strategies to tackle problems and real-world applications. Throughout the years, as attempts have been made to concentrate and manage the complexity of studying various aspects of mathematical problem solving, research attention has been redirected to mathematical modeling (Lesh and Zawojewski 2007; Lester and Kehle 2003). According to Henry Pollak:

> Problem solving may not refer to the outside world at all. Even when it does, problem solving usually begins with the idealized real-world situation in mathematical terms, and ends with a mathematical result. Mathematical modeling, on the other hand, begins in the 'unedited' real world, requires problem formulating before problem solving, and once the problem is solved, moves back into the real world where the results are considered in their original context. (Pollak 2011)

CCSS suggests that instruction in mathematics integrate modeling in mathematical tasks and activities, and they identify specific standards for which modeling is recommended, thus challenging teachers, curriculum developers, and textbook authors to bring authentic, real-world data into the classroom. Through mathematical problem solving and modeling, students' experience in mathematics will extend beyond traditional, routine word problems.

Recently, with its Essential Understanding (NCTM 2010–13) and Focus in High School Mathematics (NCTM 2009–11) series, the NCTM has offered ideas to help teachers actively involve students in analyzing and solving problems. The Implementing the Common Core State Standards through Mathematical Problem Solving series begun with this volume contributes to these efforts, specifically supporting the connections between CCSS and mathematical problem solving.

The authors of this book, Theresa Gurl, Alice Artzt, and Alan Sultan, are gratefully acknowledged for sharing their insights and ideas to help secondary mathematics teachers meet the challenges of implementing the CCSS. Thanks are due to the NCTM Educational Materials Committee for making the development of this manuscript possible, and to Joanne Hodges, Senior Director of Publications; Myrna Jacobs, Publications Manager; and the NCTM publications staff for their guidance, advice, and technical support in the preparation of the manuscript.

Frances R. Curcio
Series Editor

Preface

The high school curriculum provides rich opportunities for students to learn and do mathematics through problem solving. High school students, as they become ready for college and other postsecondary opportunities, are ready for complex and real-life situations, and they are increasingly able to extract abstract ideas from real-life applications. As stated in *Principles and Standards for School Mathematics:* "In high school, students' repertoires of problem-solving strategies expand significantly because students are capable of employing more complex methods and their abilities to reflect on their knowledge and act accordingly have grown" (NCTM 2000, p. 334).

Building on NCTM recommendations (NCTM 2011), the Common Core State Standards for Mathematics (CCSSM) further develop the standards for how students should go about doing mathematics, and thus include standards for "mathematical practice" in addition to standards for "mathematical content." Teachers have the new challenge of maintaining an environment conducive to problem solving in their classrooms while meeting the requirements of the CCSSM. The purpose of this book is to guide high school teachers in their efforts to implement these standards, both for mathematical content and for mathematical practice. As the title suggests, our emphasis here is on meeting the standards through a problem-solving approach, not only as a means of practicing what has been learned but also as a tool to "build new mathematical knowledge" (NCTM 2000, p. 52). Overall, the Common Core State Standards for Mathematics are well suited for a problem-solving approach.

To develop mathematical problem-solving skills and to support the Common Core State Standards, we highlight two approaches. First, rich problems are presented that provide a starting point for lessons, and not just an opportunity to practice what has already been learned. Our hope is that teachers will use these problems to launch lessons and allow the embedded mathematics to be revealed through classroom discourse. The second approach presents a carefully designed series of expressions and questions that allow mathematical ideas to emerge. Not every section has an equal treatment of the two approaches, as certain concepts and problems lend themselves differently to each.

This book, containing forty-four tasks, is organized mainly by the major content areas for the high school Common Core standards, with a chapter for each: Algebra, Functions, Geometry, Statistics and Probability, and Number and Quantity. Modeling does not have its own chapter, as it is represented across all of the content areas, and explicit reference is made to it where appropriate. Each chapter is organized by the domains of the CCSSM, with a section including a problem or several problems for each domain and targeting specific clusters of standards. Each problem is labeled as a "Task."

Although every domain required of all students is represented, not every standard or cluster is represented, and only interesting problems that lend themselves to meaningful implementation of content standards have been included. Our intent was not to be exhaustive, but to present exemplary problems as models for teachers. At the end of each section, the Standards for Mathematical Practice best met by the problems in the section are discussed. Although the temptation for busy teachers may be only to look at the tasks themselves, we hope that teachers also read the discussion of the problems, where we provide ideas for implementation of the tasks, possible modifications of the tasks, and common misconceptions related to the concepts inherent in the tasks.

This book is intended for use by high school mathematics teachers to support a traditional text for students, providing a source for rich problems to motivate and launch lessons as well as to exemplify mathematics learning through problem solving. In many cases, suggestions for modifying or extending the problems are given so that instruction may be differentiated. Teacher educators may use this book as a supplemental text in a methods course or a curriculum course for preservice teachers in secondary mathematics. This would help preservice teachers become familiar with the Common Core State Standards for Mathematics and how they may be implemented. Finally, teachers should find the "CCSS Overview for Middle and High School Mathematics," located in the appendix, helpful in providing a "vertical" overview of the major content areas and how they are emphasized through the middle and high school grades.

Chapter 1
Algebra

T he word *algebra* can be traced back to the year 830, when an astronomer named Mohammed ibn Musa al-Khowârizmi wrote a treatise entitled *Al-jabr w'al muqâbala*. Originally from the Arabic *al-jabr*, algebra meant "restoring" (that is, balancing) an equation, and *al-muqâbala* meant "simplification," as in combining like terms (Kline 1972). Although algebra has taken on various nonmathematical meanings throughout the centuries, today we find it as an important component of the curriculum. The development of algebraic thinking begins informally as early as the primary grades (Curcio and Schwartz 1997; NCTM 2008), and as students progress through the grades, a formal treatment of algebra occurs through pattern recognition, generalizations, variables, and functions.

The high school algebra standards are partitioned into four domains: (1) seeing structure in expressions, (2) arithmetic with polynomials and rational expressions, (3) creating equations, and (4) reasoning with equations and inequalities. As mentioned in the Preface, we employ two approaches in this book to develop mathematical problem-solving skills and support the Common Core State Standards. First, we present rich problems that give a starting point for lessons; and second, we provide a series of expressions and questions that are designed to allow mathematical ideas to emerge. In this chapter, you will find tasks to support all four domains of the algebra standards: seeing structure in expressions (tasks 1.1 and 1.2), arithmetic with polynomials and rational expressions (tasks 1.3 and 1.4), creating equations and modeling (task 1.5), and reasoning with equations and inequalities (tasks 1.6, 1.7, and 1.8). The eight Standards for Mathematical Practice (MP) (as listed on page vi) are interwoven throughout these domains. For each task, we will discuss those standards that are most relevant to the problem at hand.

Seeing Structure in Expressions

The Seeing Structure in Expressions domain of the high school algebra standards encourages students to solve problems using the structural attributes of mathematical expressions. An examination of the relationships among the graphic, algebraic, and concrete area models of quadratic expressions of the form $ax^2 + bx + c$, and of related equations $ax^2 + bx + c = 0$ or $y = ax^2 + bx + c$, provides an opportunity for deep understanding of their underlying mathematical structure. For example, when a quadratic expression is factorable, it can be modeled as a rectangle using algebra tiles (fig. 1.1), and the graph of the associated parabola will intersect the x-axis at rational points (fig. 1.2). If it is a perfect square trinomial, it can be modeled as a square using algebra tiles (fig. 1.3), and its associated parabola will be tangent to the x-axis (fig. 1.4). If it is not factorable, it cannot be modeled by a rectangle (fig. 1.5), and its associated parabola will either not intersect the x-axis or will intersect at irrational values (fig. 1.6).

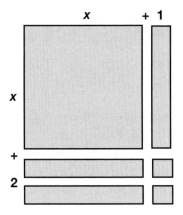

Fig. 1.1. How we can factor $x^2 + 3x + 2$ into $(x + 1)(x + 2)$

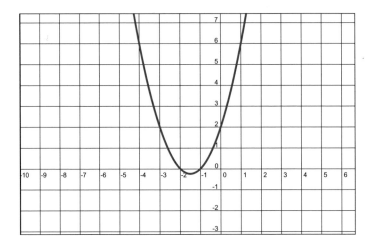

Fig. 1.2. The graph of $y = x^2 + 3x + 2$

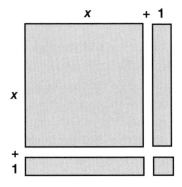

Fig. 1.3. How we can factor $x^2 + 2x + 1$ into $(x + 1)(x + 1)$ or $(x + 1)^2$

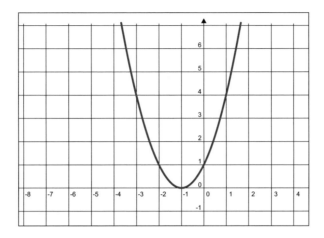

Fig. 1.4. The graph of $y = x^2 + 2x + 1$

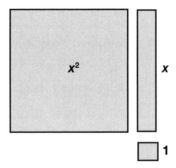

Fig. 1.5. The pieces of $x^2 + x + 1$ cannot be combined to make a rectangle, so $x^2 + x + 1$ is not factorable.

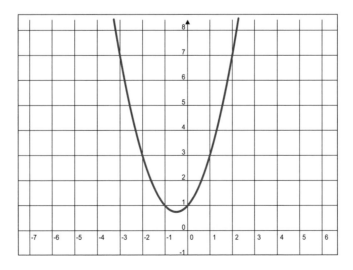

Fig. 1.6. The graph of $y = x^2 + x + 1$

Task 1.1 is intended as an introduction to these ideas, and it addresses standard A-SSE.2: "Use the structure of an expression to identify ways to rewrite it" (CCSSI 2010, p. 64). Specifically, students are asked to make observations about the resulting polynomial and its coefficients when carefully selected binomials are multiplied, leading to insight about factoring certain polynomial expressions. We encourage using the language of "distributive property" or "distribution" to describe the procedure of multiplying binomials rather than the commonly used but easily misinterpreted FOIL (First, Outer, Inner, Last) acronym. The task includes five sets of examples so that teachers may use a cooperative learning approach, but teachers may decide that fewer sets are necessary. If a cooperative learning approach is used, groups can each be given a different set, and teachers can help students compile and compare their results.

Task 1.1

(*a*) Multiply each pair of factors. How are the terms in the resulting polynomial related to the terms in the factors? Make at least two conjectures.

Set 1: $(x + 3)(x + 4)$; $(x + 3)(x - 4)$; $(x - 3)(x + 4)$; $(x - 3)(x - 4)$

Set 2: $(x + 1)(x + 5)$; $(x + 1)(x - 5)$; $(x - 1)(x + 5)$; $(x - 1)(x - 5)$

Set 3: $(x + 3)(x + 3)$; $(x + 3)(x - 3)$; $(x - 3)(x + 3)$; $(x - 3)(x - 3)$

Set 4: $(x + 10)(x + 8)$; $(x + 10)(x - 8)$; $(x - 10)(x + 8)$; $(x - 10)(x - 8)$

Set 5: $(2x + 3)(x + 5)$; $(2x + 3)(x - 5)$; $(2x - 3)(x + 5)$; $(2x - 3)(x - 5)$

(*b*) Test your conjectures by writing another set of binomials. See whether you can accurately predict the product of each pair of binomials in your set.

(*c*) What factors were multiplied to result in each of the polynomials below? Explain how the observations you made in part (*a*) would help you to figure this out.

$x^2 + 6x - 7$

$x^2 - 6x - 7$

$2x^2 + 15x + 7$

When assigning the problem in task 1.1, teachers might consider using a recording sheet so that students can make comparisons within and across examples. The design of this problem reveals the structure of expressions by allowing for a comparison of the binomials to the resulting trinomial. Students must carefully examine the structure of the terms of the binomials and the trinomial to accurately determine their relationship. Students should notice that when multiplying $(x + a)(y + b)$ the x-coefficient of the resulting polynomial is $a + b$ and the constant is ab. Teachers and students can discuss the more complicated relationship that results when the leading coefficient is not equal to one.

This approach can be extended to polynomials that are the difference of two perfect squares and trinomials that are squares of binomials. For example, several sets of binomials of the form $(x + a)(x + a)$; $(x + a)(x − a)$; $(x − a)(x + a)$; and $(x − a)(x − a)$ might be given to students, leading to factoring such polynomials as $x^2 − a^2$ or $x^2 + 2ax + a^2$.

A more concrete approach is presented in task 1.2 below, where students are asked to "make rectangles" out of the concrete representations of polynomials, revealing the relationship between factorable quadratics and the existence of a concrete rectangular model of a quadratic. Students should have some familiarity with the structure of algebra tiles before attempting this task. Note that we have only included positive coefficients because it is often counterproductive to spend time on the somewhat cumbersome representation of negative terms using a concrete area model.

Task 1.2

Using algebra tiles, form a rectangle to represent each of the following expressions, and then answer the questions that follow.

     (1) $x^2 + 7x + 10$

     (2) $x^2 + 11x + 10$

     (3) $x^2 + 7x + 12$

     (4) $x^2 + 7x + 16$

     (5) $x^2 + 11x + 5$

(*a*) In which cases were you able to model the trinomial using a rectangle? Explain why you think certain trinomials did not "work."

(*b*) Factor each trinomial above. If a trinomial is not able to be factored, explain why.

(*c*) Create a trinomial that can be modeled using a rectangle, and create a trinomial that cannot be modeled using a rectangle. Make a conjecture about the factors of each of your trinomials.

(*d*) Create a trinomial that can be modeled using a square. What do you notice about the factors of this trinomial?

STANDARDS *for Mathematical Practice—Tasks 1.1 and 1.2*

Several of the CCSS Standards for Mathematical Practice (in particular, standards 1, 4, 6, and 7) are addressed by these two problems, which first ask students to conjecture, then to test, and eventually to apply what they have discovered.

MP.1

The structure and nature of these problems allow students to make sense of the mathematics, and through the use of concrete models, persevere in solving them. Students analyze given information, make and test conjectures, and consider analogous problems of their own making, thereby "monitor[ing] and evaluat[ing] their progress" in solving each problem (CCSSI 2010, p. 6).

MP.4

Although students are not modeling a real-life situation, task 1.2 requires that they model a mathematical expression using an area model, which allows for insight into the underlying structure of the mathematics. The structure of this task allows students to "analyze relationships mathematically to draw conclusions," in this case regarding the structure of the expressions (CCSSI 2010, p. 7).

MP.6

When multiplying the binomials in task 1.1, students must make sure their calculations are correct, and thus the problem supports the sixth Standard for Mathematical Practice, "Attend to precision" (CCSSI 2010, p. 7). If the factors are not multiplied carefully, erroneous conjectures will result. Indeed, there is a self-checking feature built into the problem. If students make an error and a product does not seem to follow the same pattern as the others, it is hoped that they would find the error.

MP.7

These tasks support development of mathematically proficient students by requiring them to "look closely to discern a pattern or structure" in the sets of binomials and their products in task 1.1, thus addressing the seventh Standard for Mathematical Practice, "Look for and make use of structure" (CCSSI 2010, p. 8). Task 1.2 requires that students examine how the coefficients relate to whether the trinomial can be modeled by a rectangle. As recommended by this standard, "They can see complicated things, such as some algebraic expressions, as single objects or as being composed of several objects" (CCSSI 2010, p. 8). The structure of the tasks requires students to compare equivalent expressions in different forms (e.g., a trinomial can be expressed as the product of two binomials).

Arithmetic with Polynomials and Rational Expressions

This domain of the high school algebra standards requires that students perform arithmetic operations on polynomial and rational expressions. The following problem addresses standard A-APR.7: "Understand that rational expressions form a system analogous to the rational numbers, closed under addition, subtraction, multiplication, and division by a nonzero rational expression; add, subtract, multiply, and divide rational expressions" (CCSSI 2010, p. 65). Specifically, task 1.3 requires that students interpret a real-life situation that leads to a mathematical model in which two rational expressions need to be combined using an arithmetic operation. Students are required to express the result in simplest form to ensure that the arithmetic operation is performed on the rational expression.

Task 1.3

Ms. A's class has decided to buy her a gift. They found the perfect item at the store, and it costs G dollars. The students in the class agree to split the cost equally. The next day, ten students decide that they cannot contribute. Write an algebraic expression for the additional amount the other students had to contribute to buy the same gift.

(*a*) What quantities do we know? How might they be represented? Which need to be represented by a variable?

(*b*) Decide which quantities need to be represented by an algebraic expression, and write the expressions.

(*c*) Write an expression for the difference in price. Make sure it is in simplest form.

A teacher may elect to give the above problem without the scaffolding provided in parts (*a*), (*b*), and (*c*). Students might be asked to think about the questions that could be asked about this problem in order to solve it. This would require careful monitoring of students as they work, with teachers prompting student thought through questioning, including a discussion of the minimum number of students that must be in the class. Another modification of the problem would be to give a numerical value for the cost of the gift, the number of students in the class, or both. This simpler version of the problem could precede either version of the problem as given above. If a teacher elects to give specific values, students could be given, or be encouraged to construct, a recording table or chart to organize their findings.

The algebra standards also require that students perform arithmetic operations on polynomials. The problem that follows has an open-ended approach that allows many—in fact, infinitely many—answers to the questions, and it encourages students to critique the reasoning of others. Task 1.4 addresses cluster A-APR, "Perform arithmetic operations on polynomials" (CCSSI 2010, p. 64).

Task 1.4

The perimeter of a rectangle is represented by $4x + 24$. In response to the question, "What is a possible representation of the area of this rectangle?" Mark says, "$x^2 + 36$," and Sarah says, "No, $x^2 + 12x + 36$." What assumptions are both Mark and Sarah making about the rectangle? Comment on their answers. Other students are also discussing the problem. Alex says the area is $24x$. Anna says that she thinks the area is $x^2 + 12x + 27$. Where do you think they are getting these answers? Can they all be correct?

This problem has many correct answers and can lead to a rich discussion of the relationship between perimeter and area alongside the discussion of polynomials. An extension of this problem and/or an opportunity for differentiated instruction is to have students try to find different possible areas that have not yet been mentioned, including those that meet specific requirements, such as another that is a monomial (another is actually not possible), binomial, and trinomial. It is more challenging to find three different areas that are trinomials than ones that are binomials. Furthermore, teachers can change the initial given perimeter in ways that make the problem more or less challenging. For example, an initial perimeter of $3x + 7$ might be very challenging when students realize that rational expressions must be involved. Finally, students might be given an area that is impossible given the constraints of the problem: "Is the area $3x^2 + 72x$ possible? Why or why not?"

The problem can be extended by using various figures, such as right triangles or right trapezoids. The added challenge for these problems is that not all arrangements of sides "make sense," and that some measures are not used when calculating area.

STANDARDS *for Mathematical Practice—Tasks 1.3 and 1.4*

In order to solve the problem in task 1.3 successfully, students must carefully analyze the information given and make decisions regarding the approach they will use, including whether to use specific information (e.g., a numerical quantity for the price or number of students) to make sense of the general form. In the problem, students are told that the price of the gift can be represented by G, but need to define a variable themselves to represent the number of students in the class. For the purposes of this discussion, the number of students in the class will be represented by N. The problem in task 1.3 supports several of the Standards for Mathematical Practice (i.e., standards 1, 3, 4, and 7).

MP.1 and MP.4

Similar to tasks 1.1 and 1.2 in the previous section, task 1.3 supports the goal for mathematically proficient students to "make sense of problems and persevere in solving them" (CCSSI 2010, p. 6), by creating a situation where students need to explain "to themselves the meaning of a problem and look for entry points to its solution" (CCSSI 2010, p. 6). This is particularly true in the less scaffolded approach to the problem. Students must also be comfortable with modeling each student's contribution to the cost of the gift. With all of the students participating, each contribution is G/N, and with ten fewer students participating the cost per student becomes $G/(N-10)$. The additional amount each student would need to pay is thus modeled by the difference $G/(N-10) - G/N$. When expressing the difference in simplest form, students must find a common denominator in order to combine the fractions. Teachers can assign a specific value for either one of the variables in the problem, G or N. For example, if we allow the number of students in the class to be, say, $N = 25$, then the difference is $G/15 - G/25$, allowing for finding a common denominator without variables, but still requiring the manipulation of the variable in the numerator.

If, however, teachers elect to give a specific value for the price of the gift, this would allow for a numerical value in the numerator of each fraction, while requiring students to find the common denominator involving variables. For example, if the price of the gift is, say, $G = 50$, and there are N students, the difference is $50/(N-10) - 50/N$, requiring students to find the common denominator of $N-10$ and N. The rational expressions above are all mathematical models of the situation, addressing the fourth standard for mathematical practice. What begins as a real-life situation, one that many students may have once been in themselves, leads to a mathematical model that is a rational expression.

MP.3

In order to respond successfully to this question, students must first analyze the problem, realize that Mark and Sarah are assuming that the rectangle is a square, identify the error in Mark's multiplication, and then construct a response critiquing the incorrect answer and explaining the correct one. While Mark and Sarah's assumption that the rectangle is square is not incorrect, it certainly is not a requirement, and students must realize that other rectangles must be considered, as in the responses of Alex and Anna. Students must then realize not only that the answers provided by Alex and Anna are both mathematically correct, but that there are many (in fact, infinitely many) additional possible expressions of the area of the rectangle. In solving this problem students should be constructing viable arguments and critiquing the reasoning of others as emphasized in MP.3, part of which states: "Mathematically proficient students are also able to compare the effectiveness of two plausible arguments, distinguish correct logic or reasoning from that which is flawed, and—if there is a flaw in an argument—explain what it is" (CCSSI 2010, p. 7). In explaining that both answers are correct, and that there are other correct ones, students develop mathematical proficiency.

MP.7

This task supports the development of mathematically proficient students "who look for and make use of structure" in mathematics (CCSSI 2010, p. 8). In comparing how to add the rational expressions in the task to adding fractions with numerical values encountered in earlier grades, students must make use of the related but more complicated structure of the rational expressions, including finding a common denominator. In particular, finding the common denominator when the denominators are numerical values (i.e., when the number of students in the class is a specific value) can be compared to doing so when the number of students is represented by a variable, allowing for a structural comparison of finding a common denominator when dealing with constants to finding one when working with variables in the denominator.

Task 1.4 not only supports the development of mathematically proficient students in a similar way to task 1.3, but it also provides an opportunity for students to "construct viable arguments and critique the reasoning of others" (CCSSI 2010, p. 6).

Creating Equations

This domain of the high school algebra standards addresses students' ability to "create equations that describe numbers or relationships" (CCSSI 2010, p. 65). Task 1.5 addresses standards A-CED.2 and A-CED.3 which challenge students to "Create equations in two or more variables to represent relationships between quantities," and "Represent constraints by equations or inequalities, and by systems of equations and/or inequalities, and interpret solutions as viable or non-viable options in a modeling context" (CCSSI 2010, p. 65). Specifically, task 1.5 asks students to interpret a situation involving a business that is modeled by a quadratic function. Students are required to analyze the constraints of the problem, determine appropriate domain and range values for the function, and, if using technology, to determine an appropriate window to graph the function. A recording sheet might be provided to students, or students might be encouraged to determine their own way to organize the data. Note that the numbers are quite large by design, so that the problem is realistic.

Task 1.5

Mr. Yates makes and sells 1,000 of his new JPads per week at a cost of 350 dollars per unit. Because the demand is high, he has decided to raise the price of the JPad, but he is only considering raises in five-dollar increments. Market research has shown that for each five-dollar rise in the price, ten fewer customers are expected to buy the JPad. Thus, if the price is 355 dollars per JPad (an increase of only one five-dollar increment) only 990 customers are expected to buy the item (ten fewer than 1,000). If the price of the JPad is set at 360 dollars (going up two five-dolllar increments), then only 980 customers will buy it. Assuming that the market research is correct:

(*a*) Find the number of people who will be expected to buy the item if the price is raised to 375 dollars per unit. What will be Mr. Yates's expected weekly income?

(*b*) Compute the weekly income for several different prices of the item.

(*c*) Model the weekly income obtained if *x* five-dollar increments are added to the initial price of 350 dollars. That is, write a function to model the problem.

(*d*) Graph the resulting function from part (*c*). What does it look like?

(*e*) What should Mr. Yates charge for the item for him to realize his maximum weekly income?

As mentioned earlier, the numbers in this problem are quite large, first to render the problem as realistic, and also to provide an opportunity for students to approach the problem analytically. For example, students can write the equation for the axis of symmetry to algebraically determine the turning point of the graph, which represents the maximum income. As written, the maximum value occurs at the point (15, 361250). This means that the weekly income is maximized when the price is increased by fifteen five-dollar increments (the item will cost $425), and the number of items sold in a week will be decreased by fifteen increments of ten (selling 850), for an income of $425 \times 850 = \$361,250$. The problem can be adjusted to have a non-integral *x*-value for the turning point, which has no meaning in the function, since it is not possible to have a fractional number of increments. For example, we can decrease the number of JPads sold by nine (instead of ten) for each price increase of $5, leading to the function $C(x) = (350 + 5x)(1{,}000 - 9x)$. The turning point of this graph takes place at the point where $x = 20.56$, so students need to determine whether 20.56 or 20 or 21 is a more sensible answer in the context of the problem. If the turning point is not integral, but the answer must be an integer, the maximum can occur at either the integer to the left of the turning point or the one to the right. So we need to check both. It is also possible to make other adjustments to the problem. Teachers might change the initial cost, or the number of items sold per week to extend the problem.

A question that many teachers have is whether or not to allow students to "struggle" with mathematics, and when to provide help or intervention. Often, our intervention as teachers renders the problem much easier with lower cognitive demand than the problem as it was written. Through careful scaffolding, without giving too much information, teachers can still make sure students do not become frustrated with their work. Further, students should have the opportunity to ask questions themselves. Therefore, before providing parts (*a*), (*b*), (*c*), and (*d*) above, students could be asked to write their own questions about the situation.

STANDARDS *for Mathematical Practice—Task 1.5*

This problem supports the development of mathematically proficient students by addressing several of the CCSS Standards for Mathematical Practice (i.e., standards 4, 5, and 6).

MP.4

Task 1.5 requires students to model with mathematics, including identifying "important quantities in a practical situation" and mapping their relationships using graphs, tables, diagrams, and functions (CCSSI 2010, p. 7). In order to solve this problem, students must analyze the quantities in the problem, first by organizing the data in a table, and then by writing, graphing, and analyzing the function that represents the data. When the function is written in the form $C(x) = (350 + 5x)(1,000 - 10x)$, it is evident what the quantities represent. The first binomial represents the initial price with five-dollar increments added, and the second represents the number of items that will be sold, decreased in increments of ten dollars. In this form, however, it might not be evident to students that the function is quadratic, and students might not easily be able to determine the maximum profit in this form. Multiplying the binomials to express the function as $C(x) = -50x^2 + 1,500x + 350,000$ allows for easier substitution into the formula for the axis of symmetry, $x = -b/(2a)$. The discussion of the domain values that make sense for the model supports the development of mathematically proficient students who "routinely interpret their mathematical results in the context of the situation and reflect on whether the results make sense, possibly improving the model if it has not served its purpose" (CCSSI 2010, p. 7). Students should consider why the number of five-dollar increments cannot be more than 100. Similarly, negative numbers are not part of the domain of this problem. In fact, fractions are not part of the domain of the function in context. This can be discussed in the context of the situation discussed above, where the turning point is a non-integral value.

The scenario is one that students can imagine might arise in business, and they would be motivated to solve it in order to answer questions about the amount of money earned. Computer software may be used to model the problem, and then the students can interpret the model.

MP.5

Students must "use appropriate tools strategically" if using a graphing tool to represent the function (CCSSI 2010, p. 7). When using the standard window on most graphing tools, students will not "see" the graph, and they will need to make sense of the domain values and the function values in order to produce an appropriate graph using technology, thus analyzing "graphs of functions and solutions generated using a graphing calculator" (CCSSI 2010, p. 7; see fig. 1.7). The appropriate viewing window is certainly not evident at first attempt, and the students might erroneously conclude that the graph is a vertical line that the function resembles when an inappropriate viewing window is used. The "table" feature of a graphing utility is also useful for determining the maximum profit.

MP.6

In order to solve this problem, students must "attend to precision" (CCSSI 2010, p. 7). To make sense of the problem they must be "careful about specifying units of measure, and labeling axes to clarify the correspondence with quantities in a problem" (CCSSI 2010, p. 7).

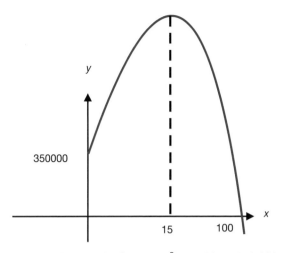

Fig. 1.7. The graph of $y = -50x^2 + 1,500x + 350,000$

Reasoning with Equations and Inequalities

Solving equations and systems of equations has long been a large part of the high school mathematics curriculum. Rich connections can be made when problems allow students to see the important relationship between graphic and algebraic relationships of equations in two variables. The following two problems are designed to allow students to make these connections while supporting the goals of the CCSS.

The intention of task 1.6 is to allow students to develop an intuitive sense of the relationship between an arithmetic "rule" and the graph of pairs of numbers that satisfy the rule (see fig. 1.8). This task might be used as a launch into a lesson on graphing linear equations.

Task 1.6

The sum of two numbers is 10. List several pairs of numbers that satisfy this requirement. If each pair of numbers is considered as an ordered pair on the coordinate plane and graphed, what do you notice about the set of graphed points? What if you continue plotting points that follow the same pattern, and write down their coordinates? What is the relationship between the coordinates? What if one of the numbers is negative? A fraction? A negative fraction? Greater than 10?

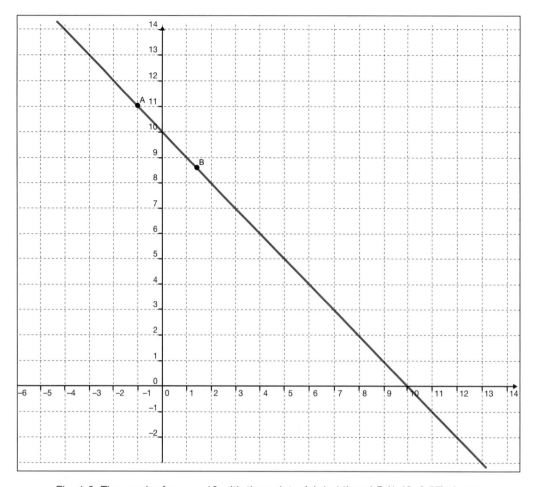

Fig. 1.8. The graph of $x + y = 10$ with the points A $(-1, 11)$ and B $(1.43, 8.57)$ shown

As discussed previously, the intention of this problem is for students to begin to notice the linear relationship of the points that satisfy the "rule." Note that no mention has yet been made of equations, slope, or y-intercept. Students should be given further examples, following a similar structure to the above task, with a variety of rules such as "the first number is three more than the second" or "the first number is one more than twice the second." After examining the pairs of coordinate points that satisfy each rule and establishing the linear relationships of the plotted points, the equations for each line, along with the notions of slope and y-intercept, could be introduced. Such technology as graphing calculators can facilitate the development of slope and y-intercept, and the effect each has on the graph of a line.

An effort should also be made to work with equations of lines parallel to the *x*-axis or *y*-axis. The graphs of these equations can be developed by asking students to write a list of coordinates that follow a given "rule" such as "the *y*-coordinate is always 5" or "the *x*-coordinate is always –3," leading to the equations $y = 5$ and $x = -3$, respectively.

The approach of listing and graphing sets of coordinates that satisfy a given rule can eventually be used to develop the idea of a system of two linear equations. A second constraint may be added to the original problem such as "In addition to having a sum of 10, the first number must be three more than the second number," allowing for the development of a second equation that may be graphed. Of course, there are other constraints that might be used, such as "the first number must be four times the second."

Task 1.7 is intended to introduce the notion of inequalities in two variables. It is designed to build on the conceptual base established in the previous task, while bringing in the notion of inequality.

Task 1.7

The sum of two numbers is *less than* 10. List as many pairs of numbers as you can that satisfy this requirement. If each pair of numbers is considered as an ordered pair on the coordinate plane and graphed, what do you notice about the set of graphed points? Can 10 be one of the numbers? Can one of the numbers be larger than 10? How can we represent *all* of the numbers whose sum is less than 10?

Similar to task 1.6, the intention of this problem is to allow students to develop an intuitive understanding of the notion of an inequality in two variables. While plotting points in which the sum of the *x*- and *y*-coordinates is less than 10, students should be encouraged to examine a wide variety of points, including points that include a negative coordinate, a fractional coordinate, and other numbers that would help to reveal the pattern of coordinates whose sum is less than 10. Further questions should be asked, including "What if the sum is less than or equal to 10?" Other examples should be given, such as "the first number is greater than twice the second" or "the first number is less than four more than the second." At this point, when the idea of a solution region is conceptually solidified, the notions of shading, and the convention of using a broken line for strict inequalities can be introduced.

STANDARDS *for Mathematical Practice—Tasks 1.6 and 1.7*

This conceptual development of equations and inequalities in two variables supports the development of mathematically proficient students by allowing students to make connections among algebraic, verbal, and graphic representations of mathematical relationships, supporting two of the Standards for Mathematical Practice (i.e., standards 6 and 7).

MP.6

Unless students graph precisely and carefully, their graphs will not reveal the linear nature of the relationships between the numbers that follow the given rule. Coordinate axes must be set up and labeled carefully, and students should realize that arrows must be used to indicate the infinite nature of the graphs of the lines. Attending to precision ensures that the solution is complete and expresses the infinite number of solutions.

MP.7

Tasks 1.6 and 1.7 provide a rich opportunity for students to "look for and make use of structure" by carefully examining the graphic representation of points that satisfy a particular arithmetic rule (CCSSI 2010, p. 8). When examining the pairs of numbers that have a sum of 10, students will likely begin with pairs of positive integers that "work," for example $1 + 9$, $2 + 8$, and so on. It might be surprising, however, when students see that $0.2 + 9.8$ and $-6 + 16$ also follow the same pattern when graphed, revealing the linear structure of the relationship. As students move to the inequality, they notice that the solution is a region that is bounded by and may or may not include the associated linear equation. This structure allows us to be able to graph any linear inequality using a similar approach.

Task 1.8 is intended to help students extend the procedure of solving quadratic equations by completing the square to its generalization, the quadratic formula. Algebra tiles may be used to begin to develop the algorithm of completing the square. For example, students can examine the constant that would need to be added to each of the following expressions in order to create a perfect square trinomial:

$$x^2 + 2x + \underline{\quad}$$
$$x^2 + 4x + \underline{\quad}$$
$$x^2 + 6x + \underline{\quad}$$
$$x^2 + 5x + \underline{\quad}$$

Algebra tiles may be used to create an area model for each, and to decide which constant would need to be added in each case to create a square. In the last example, students would need to think about how to work with the odd coefficient of x. When students become comfortable with how to solve quadratics by completing the square, the following task may be given to students. The set of equations in task 1.8 is designed to lead to the quadratic formula.

Task 1.8

Solve each of the following by completing the square:

(a) $2x^2 + 6x + 1 = 0$

(b) $2x^2 + 6x + c = 0$

(c) $2x^2 + bx + c = 0$

(d) $ax^2 + bx + c = 0$

What do you notice about each of the solutions? Do any patterns emerge? How can the solution to part (*d*) help us?

This sequence of equations solved by completing the square is designed for students to see a remarkable result: When one solves the general form of a quadratic equation by completing the square, we obtain a formula that can be used to solve all such equations—the quadratic formula. The main difficulties in this activity are the somewhat messy calculations that are required. Carefully selected problems related to adding fractions and simplifying radicals might be given as a precursor to this exercise. This task is designed to address CCSS A-REI.4a: "Use the method of completing the square to transform any quadratic equation in *x* into an equation of the form $(x - p)^2 = q$ that has the same solutions. Derive the quadratic formula from this form" (CCSSI 2010, p. 65). While deriving the formula, students may notice that there are several ways to express "the answer," leading to a discussion about why the current form is used (see fig. 1.9). For example, why was the decision made to express the formula as one fraction rather than two?

$$x = \frac{-b \pm \sqrt{b^2 - 4ac}}{2a}$$

Fig. 1.9. The quadratic formula

STANDARDS *for Mathematical Practice—Task 1.8*

Two of the Standards for Mathematical Practice (i.e., standards 6 and 7) are supported by task 1.8.

MP.6

Because of the algorithmic nature of completing the square, and the potential for arithmetic error in manipulating the general coefficients, students must be very careful when working on this task, thus attending to precision. A seemingly small error in combining fractions or simplifying radicals will lead to an erroneous result.

MP.7

The structure of mathematics plays an important role in the development of the algorithm of completing the square and the derivation of the quadratic formula. Leading up to the development of the algorithm using algebra tiles, students examine the properties of a perfect square trinomial, first concretely, and then abstractly. Students then may consider the structure of the commonly used form of the quadratic formula, and why mathematicians chose to represent it in its commonly used form.

Chapter 2

Functions

Ever since the seventeenth century when Galileo recognized its usefulness in describing the mathematics of motion (Kline 1972), the concept of function—"the keynote of Western culture" (Schaaf 1930, p. 500)—has become "an important unifying idea in mathematics" (NCTM 1989, p. 154). The phrase "function of x" is attributed to Leibniz, and the notation "$f(x)$" appeared in 1734 in Euler's work (Kline 1972). While examining patterns and the relationships between and among variables is a staple of the secondary algebra and precalculus curricula, the notion of function is embedded throughout the school mathematics curriculum.

The CCSS high school standards for functions are partitioned into four domains: (1) interpreting functions; (2) building functions; (3) linear, quadratic, and exponential models; and (4) trigonometric functions, with several clusters for each domain. The Standards for Mathematical Practice (MP) are woven throughout the problems that exemplify each of the clusters. As with the other chapters in this book, we present rich problems that may provide a starting point or launch for lessons, and an opportunity for discovery of new concepts. We will also provide suggestions for scaffolding and extending each of the problems.

What follows are eleven tasks to support interpreting functions (tasks 2.1, 2.2, 2.3, and 2.4); building functions (tasks 2.5 and 2.6); linear, quadratic, and exponential models (tasks 2.7, 2.8, and 2.9); and trigonometric functions (tasks 2.10 and 2.11). The eight Standards for Mathematical Practice are woven throughout these domains, and depending on the problem, a subset of the standards is discussed specifically wherever relevant.

Interpreting Functions

Tasks 2.1, 2.2, 2.3, and 2.4 are intended to allow students to discover and develop understanding of the concept of functions and function notation, first in the context of some practical types of questions and then in a problem that requires higher-level thinking. The Common Core State Standards that are met within these problems are under the domain of F-IF, which is Interpreting Functions. Several of the clusters in this domain are met, including F-IF.1 and F-IF.2 in the cluster "Understand the concept of a function and use function notation"; F-IF.4 and F-IF.5 in the cluster "Interpret functions that arise in applications in terms of the context"; and F-IF.7 and F-IF.8 in the cluster "Analyze functions using different representations" (CCSSI 2010, p. 69). The purpose of the following tasks is to establish an intuitive feel for the notion of function, and then work toward formalization and application. Task 2.1 uses some informal examples to allow students to examine the attributes of relationships that are functions in comparison to the attributes of relationships that are not.

Task 2.1

I. In *all* these examples (1 through 4), y is a function of x:

1. If you enter a person's name (x) in a database, there is a unique footprint (y) on file from when he or she was born.

2. When you use a vending machine, you push a certain letter (x), and your candy of choice (y) comes out.

3. A person (x) goes into a movie theater and pays the admission fee of five dollars (y). The fee is the same for everyone.

4. You visit a website where you enter the date (x) and it tells you the temperature measured at 3 p.m. at a particular weather station in Central Park on that day (y).

II. In *none* of these examples (5 through 7) is y a function of x:

5. You are planning a trip, and on your computer you enter an amount of money (x) you can spend on airfare. The computer gives you the many different places (y) you could fly to using that amount of money.

6. Your friend writes a computer program in which you enter any positive number (x) and the computer writes two (y) values, $\sqrt{x}$ and $-\sqrt{x}$.

7. You visit a website where you enter the date (x) and it tells you the high and low temperatures measured at a particular weather station in Central Park on that day (y).

III. In which of the following examples is y a function of x?

8. When you use a vending machine, you push a certain letter (x), and no matter what letter you press, one box of Krispy Crunchies (y) comes out.

9. When Ms. Smith calls a student's name (x), the student tells her each of the 10 numbers he or she rolled on a die (y).

10. When Mr. Kim calls a student's name (x), the student tells him the mean of the 10 numbers he or she rolled on a die (y).

11. You give your friend any number (x), he squares it and then adds 2 and tells you the result (y).

IV. What does it mean for y to be a function of x?

The purpose of task 2.1 is to allow students to discover, by comparing attributes of examples and non-examples of functions, that, in order for y to be a function of x for each input value (x), there is exactly one output value (y). It is important to have students work through all of parts I through IV, so that they can think through the important attributes in each example and non-example before attempting to make a conjecture in part IV. In part III, students must compare the examples to the earlier ones to determine which are and are not functions. All the examples in part III are functions except example 9. Examples 3 and 8 are intended to introduce the notion of a constant function, in which every input value gives the same output value, targeting a common misconception that input values that map to a constant value are not functions.

Task 2.2 introduces formal function notation, and it delves deeper into the concept and representation of functions. Graphic representations of functions are also introduced.

Task 2.2

(a) An apple costs 30 cents. How much do five apples cost? Ten apples?

(b) How would we represent the cost of *x* apples?

(c) "The cost of five apples is 150 cents." If we wanted to abbreviate this sentence, we could write $C(5) = 150$. What do you think $C(5)$ means in words?

(d) We read the expression $C(x)$ as "*C* of *x*." How would you read $C(15)$? What does $C(15)$ mean? What is its value?

(e) Why do mathematicians use notation like $C(15)$? Why not just write out the words?

(f) Suppose we were to set up an *x*-axis and a *y*-axis, only now the *y*-axis represents $C(x)$. Plot points $(x, C(x))$ for different values of *x*. What kind of graph do we get?

Task 2.3 allows students to determine whether particular examples are functions, introducing cases that target common misconceptions. For example, part (*a*) addresses the misconception that if two values (other than zero) map to a particular value, then the relation is not a function. Part (*b*) targets the fact that in a function, one value may not map to two different values. Parts (*c*) through (*e*) target the same ideas using arrow diagrams.

Task 2.3

(a) In mathematics, when we have two quantities *x* and *y* that are related, then we say that *y* is function of *x*, if for each *x* under consideration, there is only one *y* that is associated with it. So, for example, if *x* and *y* are related by the equation $y = x^2$ would *y* be a function of *x* if the *x*-values under consideration are $x = 1$; $x = 2$; and $x = 3$? What if the *x*-values under consideration are all numbers *x*? Explain how you are making your conclusion.

(b) If $y = \pm\sqrt{x}$ and the *x*-values under consideration are all nonnegative *x*, is *y* a function of *x*? Why?

(*c*) Figure 2.1 relates *x*-values to *y*-values. Is *y* a function of *x?* If the arrows in figure 2.1 are reversed, is *x* a function of *y?* Explain your reasoning.

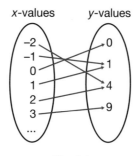

Fig. 2.1

(*d*) In figure 2.2, is *y* a function of *x?* How do you know?

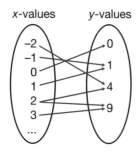

Fig. 2.2

(*e*) In figure 2.3, where *y* is a function of *x,* what is $f(-2)$? $f(3)$?

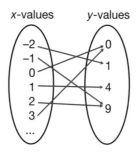

Fig. 2.3

Task 2.4 allows students to "interpret functions that arise in applications in terms of the context" (CCSSI 2010, p. 69). In particular, the domain of the functions in the abstract becomes restricted when considered within a real-life context.

Task 2.4

(*a*) Psychologists often study how fast a task is learned. In a study of the rate at which animals learn a task, hamsters were sent through a certain maze again and again, and the length of time it took them from the entrance to the exit was recorded. It was found that the time to make this trip on the *n*th trial was approximately $T(n) = 4 + 20/n$ minutes. Approximately how long did the hamster take to make the trip on the first trial? The fifth trial? The tenth? Which values of *n* make sense in the experiment?

(*b*) The government estimates that to inoculate *x* percent of the population against the latest flu virus, it will cost approximately $300x/(250 - x)$ million dollars. What is the approximate cost of inoculating 20 percent of the population? For which values of *x* does this function make practical sense? Is this expression a function of *x* for these values?

Students might note that negative numbers are part of the domains of each of the functions in (*a*) and (*b*), but they do not make sense in either context. Therefore, in these contexts, the original domains are changed. Of course, zero is not part of the domain of the first function. Without a context, the domain of the function in part (*b*) would include $x = 150$, but this value does not make sense in the real-life context of the function either, since the variable represents the percent of the population inoculated, and you cannot inoculate 150 percent of the population. Therefore, the domain must be between 0 and 100.

STANDARDS *for Mathematical Practice—Tasks 2.1 through 2.4*

The four tasks presented in this section support the Common Core State Standards (CCSS) for Mathematical Practice (as listed on page vi). In particular, students who successfully work on these problems will be meeting MP standards 2, 3, and 4.

MP.2

This standard requires that students "reason abstractly and quantitatively" (CCSSI 2010, p. 6). In particular, task 2.1 presents a variety of situations that allow students to determine the meaning of "function." They must examine the contexts of each of the scenarios to determine sensible outcomes for each. Students must be able to "contextualize" and "decontextualize." For example, the second function allows all x not equal to 250 in the domain, but the context of the problem further restricts the domain to real numbers between and inclusive of 0 and 100. Similarly, students would need to determine a sensible domain in context for the first part of task 2.4. Clearly, negative numbers do not make sense, but it should also be discussed whether very large numbers make sense; that is, can a hamster make 100 trips? 1,000? 5,000?

MP.3

In working on tasks 2.2 and 2.3, students are asked to make conjectures about the meaning of the notations being used and what they think the definition of function is. They are asked to justify their conclusion, thus "constructing viable arguments." Task 2.2 requires that they make sense out of the function notation that is being introduced and discuss the usefulness of such notation. In task 2.3 they are presented with the definition of a function. They must make sense out of this definition and then be able to apply the definition to several contexts, justifying their conclusions.

MP.4

Task 2.4 in particular allows students the opportunity to "model with mathematics." Both of the functions presented in task 2.4 model real-life situations, where students must determine sensible input or domain values. They must make a distinction between the domain of each of the functions in the abstract, and the changes to the domains in the context of the problems, thereby "interpret[ing] their mathematical results in the context of the situation and reflect[ing] on whether the results make sense" (CCSSI 2010, p. 7).

Building Functions

This section seeks to extend the notion of functions to meet the standards in the domain of F-BF, Building Functions, including F-BF.1 and F-BF.3 in the clusters "Build a function that models a relationship between two quantities" and "Build new functions from existing functions" (CCSSI 2010, p. 70). As a result of the nature of the functions presented, these tasks also satisfy some of the standards for the domain of Linear, Quadratic, and Exponential Models (F-LE). Task 2.5 is designed to have students "write a function that models a relationship between two quantities" (CCSSI 2010, p. 70), with cost as a function of usage for a cell phone, and it asks them to combine functions using arithmetic operations. Task 2.5 may also be related to systems of equations, since students are asked to compare two linear equations that model cost.

Task 2.5

The cell phone plan that Kara has costs $50 per month plus five cents per minute. Her sister Anna's cell phone plan costs her thirty cents a minute.

(*a*) Who has the better plan? Why? What additional information might you need about Kara and Anna to answer this question?

(*b*) Write a function to model each plan. Explain how you built your functions. Use your function to evaluate the cost for each plan for talking for 50 minutes per month, 100 minutes per month, and 300 minutes per month.

(*c*) On the same set of coordinate axes, graph the functions you wrote in part (*b*), and explain how the graph helps determine who has the better plan. What is the significance of 200 minutes?

(*d*) Kara and Anna's mom is paying for the two plans. What single function can model the total monthly amount she will pay at the end of the month?

(*e*) Nicky's cell phone plan is $25 per month, plus fifty cents per call. What is different about this plan? How can it be compared with the other two plans?

The graph of the functions created in part (*c*) allows for easy comparison of plans, and for visual representation of the break-even point, relating directly to systems of equations. Students should be encouraged to write functions using formal function notation to model Kara's and Anna's plans. Teachers can spark rich discussion by building on part (*c*), and asking students to explain the criteria they might use in order to determine the better plan, allowing them to see that deciding which plan is "better" depends on number of minutes used. The break-even point occurs at $x = 200$, with Anna's plan being better for under 200 minutes of calls per month, and Kara's better for more than 200 minutes. Further, discussion of Nicky's plan in part (*e*) requires that students realize that the variable is different for a function that models this plan, as the plan is based on the number of calls instead of number of minutes. Discussion among peers and with the teacher should allow students to conclude that Nicky's plan is difficult to compare with the other two without additional information, such as how long an "average" call is. What if a person made only one 300-minute call per month? Or what if a person made 300 one-minute calls? Students can be encouraged to discuss which plans might be best in different situations. For example, suppose Andrew decides that the plan that Anna has is best for him. What can we conclude about the amount of talking that Andrew does per month?

Task 2.6 provides a problem that teachers can use as a launch for a lesson that involves composition of functions.

Task 2.6

Two workers arrive at work at 7 a.m. Worker 1 produces, on the average, $q(t) = 3t$ radios in t hours. Worker 2 produces twice as many radios per hour. The production cost of manufacturing q radios increases with the number of radios and is given by $C(q) = q^2 + q$.

(a) Create a function that expresses how many radios Worker 2 produces in t hours. Write a single function that expresses the number of radios Worker 1 and Worker 2 produce together in t hours.

(b) Express the manufacturing cost for the number of radios produced by Worker 1 after three hours, after five hours, and then after t hours. When will the manufacturing cost reach \$28,000?

This problem can be extended in several ways. Initially, students might examine the graphs of the functions for each individual worker, and then of the graph of the function for their combined productivity. If the second worker's productivity is modeled by $r(t) = 6t$, students can examine the graphs of $q(t)$, $r(t)$, and $q(t) + r(t)$ and notice the increased steepness of the graphs. A further extension might be to create a situation where a constant is added to one of the functions. For example, consider the following: "After working t hours, Worker 1 decided to finish two more radios. Write a function that gives the number of radios produced by Worker 1 under this scenario." Students could be asked to graph the function $q(t) + 2$, and then make comparisons with the graph of $q(t)$, noting that the new graph is shifted vertically +2 units.

The production cost function is quadratic. When students substitute in the function for the number of radios produced, they are finding the composition of the two functions $C(q(t))$. Although the question in part (b) asks students about the cost of production for Worker 1, they could similarly be asked to examine the production cost for Worker 2 individually, or for the total cost, substituting the $q(t) + r(t)$ into the $C(q)$ function. In part (b), students can determine when the manufacturing cost reaches \$28,000, either graphically, for an estimate of the number of hours, or algebraically, which requires the use of the quadratic formula. They might also use the "table" feature of a graphing calculator in order to solve this problem. A teacher might further modify this problem by creating a new cost function. For example, students might consider the following: *With the development of new technology, cost of production has been cut by 30 percent. Write a new function that models the new production cost.* Students can then compare $C(q)$ and $0.7C(q)$ graphically, noting the changes in the function. (Because the cost has been cut 30 percent, we pay 70 percent of the original cost.)

STANDARDS *for Mathematical Practice—Tasks 2.5 and 2.6*

As students work on the two tasks presented in this section, they will encounter standards 4 and 5 for Mathematical Practice.

MP.4

Both task 2.5 and task 2.6 provide an opportunity for students to model with mathematics. Task 2.5 allows students to examine and compare cell phone plans that are modeled using functions. Students must also make sense out of the input values, since two of the functions use number of minutes as input, while the third uses number of calls. Clearly, it is not possible to compare the third function with the other two in a straightforward way. More information is needed, such as the average length of call. This provides students with a situation in which they make "assumptions and approximations to simplify a complicated situation" (CCSSI 2010, p. 7), making changes as necessary as they progress. For example, they might assume that because Nicky's plan is based on the number of calls, each of his calls is three minutes long. However, it is important to discuss habits of usage. Perhaps Nicky only uses his cell phone to make one very long call per week. Teachers and students can work together to create other scenarios.

Similarly, task 2.6 provides the opportunity to model the cost of production based on worker productivity using the composition of two functions. Students must identify the important quantities and determine how they are related, concluding that one function must be substituted into the other. In both cases students must "identify important quantities" and analyze relationships to draw conclusions (CCSSI 2010, p. 7).

MP.5

When solving the problems in tasks 2.5 and 2.6, students must determine when it is helpful to use a graphing tool, such as a graphing calculator, or simply to create a pencil-and-paper graph. A graphic representation presents a useful visual for the break-even point when comparing the cell phone plans in task 2.5. The table function of a graphing calculator would allow for a determination of when production costs reach $28,000. Also, a graphing calculator would enable students to examine visually how the graphs of the functions change when a constant is added to or multiplied by the output value.

Linear, Quadratic, and Exponential Functions

The problems in this section are designed to address the standards under the domain of Linear, Quadratic, and Exponential Models (F-LE). In task 2.7, students examine and compare the output for linear and exponential functions, looking at the difference between a *y*-value and the previous *y*-value. This task is intended to serve as a launch for a lesson on comparing different types of functions, and addresses the cluster of standards under F-LE.1, "Distinguish between situations that can be modeled with linear functions and with exponential functions" (CCSSI 2010, p. 70).

Task 2.7

(a) Complete the missing values in table 2.1 and table 2.2.

(b) What is the pattern of the successive y-values in table 2.1? How do the y-values change as the x-values increment by 1? Is the relationship additive? Multiplicative? Other?

(c) What is the pattern of the successive y-values in table 2.2? How do the y-values change as the x-values increment by 1? Is the relationship additive? Multiplicative? Other?

(d) Create tables like the ones below for the functions $f(x) = 8 - 5x$ and $g(x) = 2.5^x$. What is the pattern of the successive y-values in each of the tables? How do the y-values change as the x-values increment by 1?

Table 2.1

x	1	2	3	4	5	6	7
$y = f(x) = 4 + 3x$	7	10	13				

Table 2.2

x	1	2	3	4	5	6	7
$y = f(x) = 2x$	2	4	8				

(e) Make a conjecture about the pattern of the successive y-values as the x-values increment by 1 for $f(x) = a + bx$ and for $g(x) = b^x$.

(f) Peter makes a table for a function $h(x)$ and notices that the y-values look like those in table 2.3. What function might $h(x)$ be? How can you test your conjecture?

Table 2.3
The y-values in Peter's table

3	9	27	81	243

Task 2.7 is designed to allow students to make conjectures about the changes in successive output values for each function. To give students more experience with this, teachers may ask students to create tables for a variety of linear and exponential functions in order to make better conclusions. Linear functions grow by adding equal amounts to successive values, while exponential functions grow by multiplying equal amounts to successive values.

 Examination of differences over equal intervals for the output of functions can help students to determine the rule for functions. Once they discover that linear functions grow by adding equal amounts to successive values and exponential functions grow by multiplying equal amounts to successive values, determining a function that fits given data becomes much easier. Task 2.8 is presented with this in mind.

Task 2.8

(a) Find a function, $f(x)$, that fits the data in table 2.4.

Table 2.4

x	$f(x)$
2	8
3	13
4	18
5	23

(b) Find a function $g(x)$ that fits the data in table 2.5.

Table 2.5

x	$g(x)$
2	1.21
3	1.331
4	1.4641
5	1.61051

By examining the successive y-values, the task of finding an appropriate function to fit each set of data becomes a bit easier. Students can examine the differences for the function values in part (a), and noticing that y-values increase by adding 5, they can conclude that the function is linear, reasoning eventually that $f(x) = 5x - 2$. Although part (b) is more difficult, students, upon examination of the successive y-values, can conclude that the function is exponential since the y-values increase by a factor of 1.1. Therefore, $g(x) = 1.1^x$.

Task 2.9 addresses F-LE.5: "Interpret expressions for functions in terms of the situation they model" (CCSSI 2010, p. 71). Its purpose is to provide some typical applications of exponential functions. Although problems like these would traditionally be used to practice applying exponential functions, we suggest using them as a launch to motivate the need for exponential functions. Before formally modeling the situations using a function, students might examine the values for each of the scenarios using a table in order to determine the ways the quantities are related before generalizing using function notation.

Task 2.9

(*a*) A bank pays 5 percent annual interest on your money, compounded annually. Assume that you put in 352 dollars and neither add nor subtract money from the account. How much will the account be worth in three years? Five years? *N* years?

(*b*) An antipollution device uses filters to remove pollutants from the air. Each filter removes 20 percent of the pollutants in the air that passes through it. If a polluted sample of air is run through a device with *n* filters, what percentage of the pollutants remain when the air sample exits the device?

(*c*) A population of bacteria doubles every twenty minutes. If we start with 100 bacteria, what will the population be after *n* hours?

The functions in task 2.9 give students the opportunity to work with and interpret examples of exponential growth and decay. In part (*a*), the interest is compounded annually, but teachers can extend the problem by asking students to calculate interest compounded monthly, weekly, or daily. Part (*b*) should spark discussion about what a realistic number of filters might be. Does the problem make sense for ten filters? Is it realistic to consider 100, or 1,000 filters?

STANDARDS *for Mathematical Practice—Tasks 2.7 through 2.9*

The three tasks in this section support the CCSS Standards for Mathematical Practice. In particular, students who successfully work on them will meet standards 4, 7, and 8.

MP.4

The problems presented in task 2.9 provide the opportunity to model a variety of scenarios using exponential models, including both those of exponential growth and decay. Students must consider the domain and range for the function in context, and they must include what values make sense in the function. Although in the abstract it might be possible to have 1,000 filters, this scenario could be considered very unlikely. This leads to the discussion of the difference in the domain of a function in the abstract as compared to a function in context.

MP.7 and MP.8

The tables presented in task 2.7 allow students to "look for and make use of structure" (CCSSI 2010, p. 8). In fact, an examination of the changes in the *y*-values provides an opportunity to examine the structural attributes of how different types of functions grow. This enables students to use the structural attributes of different types of functions to write a function rule, as in task 2.8. Closely related to the examination of structure is the mathematical practice discussed in MP.8, "Look for and express regularity in repeated reasoning" (CCSSI 2010, p. 8). In approaching task 2.9, students consider using a variety of input values, organized in table form, to determine the outcomes for each problem. In examining the values obtained by repeatedly using numerical input, students should be able to generalize the numerical output by expressing the output as a function.

Trigonometric Functions

The problems presented in this section are intended to address the domain F-TF, Trigonometric Functions (CCSSI 2010, p. 71). Task 2.10 is designed for students to discover the relationship between constants and coefficients of various parts of the functions and their graphs.

Task 2.10

I.   Compare and contrast each of the following graphs using your graphing calculator.

   (1) $F(x) = \sin x$ and $G(x) = \sin 2x$

   (2) $F(x) = 3 \sin 2x$ and $G(x) = 3 \sin 2(x - \pi/2)$

   (3) $F(x) = 3 \cos 4x$, $G(x) = -3 \cos 4x$, $H(x) = 5 - 3 \cos 4x$, and
        $M(x) = 5 - 3 \sin 4(x - \pi)$

II. Make some predictions about how the graph of $f(x) = D + A \sin B (x - C)$ changes when:

   (*a*) only *A* changes

   (*b*) only *B* changes

   (*c*) only *C* changes

   (*d*) only *D* changes

III. How can you test your predictions?

Students should be encouraged to set *A* and *B* equal to 1, and to set *C* and *D* equal to 0, and to focus on changing only one of the coefficients at a time. For example, to examine the effect of *A* on the graph, students should use *B* = 1, *C* = 0, *D* = 0, and choose a variety of values for *A*. Eventually, students should change more than one of *A*, *B*, *C*, or *D* at a time, examining the combined effect of each of the variables on the function.

The purpose of task 2.11 is to provide an opportunity for the examination of data that fits a sinusoidal pattern. Teachers should discuss with students why it can make sense in certain situations for weather data to fit a sinusoidal pattern. Students should plot the data, and then examine the amplitude in order to determine the function that best fits these data.

Task 2.11

The average temperature in Fahrenheit in each month in a certain southern town over a 29-year period from 1961 to 1990 is given in table 2.6.

Table 2.6
Average Fahrenheit temperature by month 1961–90

Jan	Feb	Mar	Apr	May	Jun	Jul	Aug	Sept	Oct	Nov	Dec
48.9	51.8	59.2	66.0	73.5	79.1	81.8	81.0	76.6	67.3	59.1	51.7

Labeling January as *x* = 0, and February as *x* = 1, and so on, model this average monthly temperature with a sine curve. That is, find *A*, *B*, *C*, and *D* so that $D + A \sin B(x - C)$ fits the data.

(*Answer:* 65.35 + 16.45 sin((π/6)(*x* – 3)), where *x* = month)

In general, when you have a sinusoidal curve, $f(x) = D + A \sin B(x - C)$, *D* is always how high the "center" point is, where the "center" point means the point on the graph that is midway between the maximum and minimum. *D* is always computed by averaging the maximum height and minimum height. In this case, *D* = ½(81.8 + 48.9) = 65.35. The value of *A* is the amplitude, and that is always the distance from the height of the center point to the height of the highest point on the graph. In this case, the distance is 81.8 – 65.36, or approximately 16.45. *C* is how far horizontally the center point is from the origin. (*C* is positive if this point is to the right of the origin, and negative otherwise.) Since the lowest point occurs at *t* = 0 and the highest point at *t* = 6, the center point is at *t* = 3. So *C* = 3. The period is the time to complete the cycle, and it is 12 (months). Since 2π /*B* is the period, 2π/*B* = 12, so *B* = π/6. So one correct answer is *f*(*x*) = 65.35 + 16.45 sin((π/6)(*x* – 3)), where *x* is the month number (see fig. 2.4).

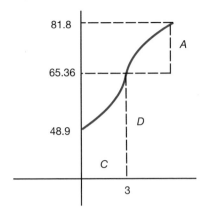

Fig. 2.4

Students could also use the calculator to fit the data by a trigonometric function. They are likely to see a function different from the one that we gave. (Calculators use a very specific algorithm to fit the data to a curve different from ours.) This should indicate that there are other ways to model the same situation, ones that also give good results.

STANDARDS *for Mathematical Practice—Tasks 2.10 and 2.11*

In task 2.10, students make some conclusions about the graphs of trigonometric functions, and they consider how changes in constants affect their graphs. In task 2.11, students use real data to graph a trigonometric function that best fits a set of data. The model can be used to predict future data points. As students successfully work on these tasks, they will meet standards 4, 5, and 7 of the Standards for Mathematical Practice.

MP.4

Given the real data in task 2.11, students are getting experience in learning to "model with mathematics" (CCSSI 2010, p. 7). Initially, teachers should discuss with students the types of cyclical data that might be modeled with a trigonometric graph. With changes in season, it should make sense that temperatures can follow a cyclic pattern over time. Once this is established, students can use the given information to plot points on the coordinate plane, allowing them to approximate the coefficients and constants that would lead to the trigonometric function that best fits the data. Also, tides vary fairly regularly within a season between high and low tide, and they can often be modeled sinusoidally. The electricity that we have in our homes is known as alternating current, and this is modeled using sinusoidal functions. Radio stations send their broadcasts along invisible waves that are also modeled sinuosoidally. The more students are made aware of how the mathematics can be used, the more willing they will be to learn it.

MP.5

Task 2.10 requires that students carefully isolate each of the four constants and coefficients in the standard form of a trigonometric function. Students "use appropriate tools strategically" (CCSSI 2010, p. 7) by using a graphing tool, such as a graphing calculator, in order to make conclusions about the effect of each of the four values on the graph individually, and then to examine their combined effect.

MP.7

By applying the generalizations discovered through task 2.10 to fitting a trigonometric function to the sinusoidal data in task 2.11, students must "look for and make use of structure" (CCSSI 2010, p. 8). Observing the structural effect of each of the four constants A, B, C, and D on the graph of a trigonometric function allows students to determine the graph that best fits the data in task 2.11.

Chapter 3
Geometry

The word *geometry* is from the Greek, *geos,* which means "earth," and *metron,* which means "measure." Geometry involves the study of shapes found in the natural world as well as those in human-made objects. When we view the world in all its shapes and dimensions, we can see geometry all around us, and this is what we hope students will be made aware of throughout the tasks in this chapter. In addition, and most important at the high school level, the underlying structures of figures are quite interesting. Fascinating questions arise in the study of geometry. For example, what are the specific features of structures that make them appear as they do? What does one have to know in order to create a certain shape? What makes certain shapes look exactly the same? What makes certain figures of different sizes have the same shape? In this chapter, we present a problem-solving approach in which the figures presented to students will arouse their curiosity and, through approaches such as measurement and logic, help them to discover the fascinating underlying relationships that exist between and among geometric figures.

The CCSS high school geometry standards are partitioned into six domains: (1) congruence; (2) similarity, right triangles, and trigonometry; (3) circles; (4) expressing geometric properties with equations; (5) geometric measurement and dimension; and (6) modeling with geometry.

What follows are seven tasks to support congruence (tasks 3.1 and 3.2), similarity (tasks 3.3 and 3.4), expressing geometric properties with equations (task 3.5), and circles (tasks 3.6 and 3.7). The eight Standards for Mathematical Practice (MP), as listed on page vi, are woven throughout these domains. Depending on the problem, a subset of the standards is discussed. We believe that all the problems require "attention to precision," thus developing mathematically proficient students as required by standard 6 of the Standards for Mathematical Practice.

Congruence

A large part of the geometry curriculum involves congruence proofs. Students often do not see the value or applicability in learning these proofs. We hope that relating the usefulness of congruent triangles to architecture will help students to see the practical value of proof. Students should understand that it is not enough that figures "appear" to be congruent, but that we need to be certain of their congruence.

Architectural structures such as a truss bridge often contain congruent triangles. You can find a wide variety of truss bridges to print out as examples simply by doing a Web image search on the phrase "truss bridge." The sketch of the structure of a truss bridge in figure 3.1 allows for easy examination of the triangles. Careful examination of pictures of actual truss bridges along with figure 3.1 can lead to a rich discussion about whether the triangles intuitively seem congruent, why this would be important in an application, and whether it is enough that they *seem* congruent. This addresses standard G-CO.8, which relates to students' envisioning congruence through such rigid motions as reflection, translation, or rotation. Students might be asked to consider the following questions, along with doing task 3.1 below, which can serve as the launch for the lesson.

- How are triangles drawn or constructed to ensure that they are congruent?

- Must all three angles and all three sides of a triangle be measured to create a second triangle congruent to the original? If not, what would be the minimum number of measurements we would have to know?

- For example, if we measured only the three sides of one triangle and created a second triangle with the sides having those same lengths, would the new triangle be congruent to the original? (Note that we have not measured any of the angles of the original triangle.)

- Consider the following similar question: If we measured only the three angles of one triangle and created a second triangle having the same angle measures, would the new triangle be congruent to the original?

- Suppose we have the measures of one angle and two sides of a triangle. If we construct a second triangle with these same measures, would the new triangle be congruent to the original?

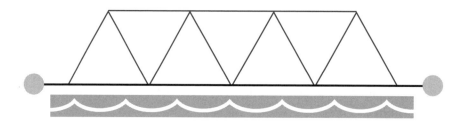

Fig. 3.1. Truss bridge diagram

Task 3.1

Using a ruler, draw a large triangle on a clean sheet of paper. Then measure the length of each of the sides of the triangle you have drawn. Using these same three lengths, try to draw another triangle that is *not* congruent to the first one you drew. Could you do it? Why or why not? (Sultan and Artzt 2010, p. 159)

Teachers might prefer to do the above activity in a more hands-on way. For example, students could be provided with manipulative materials, such as straws, and scissors to cut them into different lengths. Students would be instructed to create a triangle using the straws, and then asked to create a second triangle using three straws of the same lengths that is *not* congruent to the first one. This activity allows students to physically place the triangles together to "prove" informally that the triangles are in fact congruent. Of course, it is important to cut the straws into lengths that meet the triangle inequality criteria and in fact form a triangle! In order to avoid this problem, teachers might elect to give students specific lengths with which to work, but this detracts somewhat from the value of the activity because students might believe there is something "special" about the teacher-given lengths.

The Geometer's Sketchpad or similar dynamic geometry software might also be used for this activity. An online activity is available at NCTM's Illuminations website: http://illuminations.nctm.org/ActivityDetail.aspx?id=4.

After being unable to create a different-shaped triangle, students will begin to realize that given the lengths of three sides of a triangle, one and only one triangle can be created. This will lead to a conjecture for the theorem that if the three sides of a triangle *ABC* are congruent to the three sides of triangle *DEF,* then triangles *ABC* and *DEF* are congruent. (This theorem is referred to as SSS, for side-side-side.) Students can convince themselves using rigid motions, examining and explaining whether one triangle they created could result from the other through a translation, reflection, or a rotation, or some composition of these. Note that SSS can be proven using the law of cosines. The theorems for SAS (for side-angle-side) and ASA (for angle-side-angle) can be proven using the law of cosines and the law of sines, respectively (Sultan and Artzt 2010).

It is also important for students to determine that certain arrangements of congruent corresponding parts of a pair of triangles are *not* enough to establish congruency of the triangles. For example, AAA (angle-angle-angle) is enough only to establish similarity, and SSA (side-side-angle) is ambiguous and therefore not sufficient. Students often do not see why SSA does not establish congruency, so we have included the counterexample in figure 3.2. Given an isosceles triangle, draw *any* segment from the vertex to the base that is *not* the altitude. The resulting two triangles are clearly not congruent, even though we have SSA congruent to SSA.

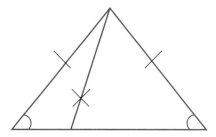

Fig. 3.2. Side-side-angle correspondence does not work for proving congruence.

Upon completion of these experiences, students should create a table indicating which arrangements of corresponding parts lead to congruence, which lead to similarity, and which do not lead to any conclusions. In each case, they should draw an example that will help them understand, recall, and synthesize the results they arrived at through their investigations.

Many students find it difficult to construct logical reasoning progressions that lead to a proof. One mistake students commonly make is assuming what it is they want to prove in their proof. Also, a frequent debate among mathematics teachers is whether or not to insist on a "two-column" proof format. Task 3.2 concerns a typical lesson on how to prove that triangles within a figure are congruent. We encourage students to analyze the figure before writing any part of the proof. For example, we ask them to decide what they might be able to prove, and how they would go about doing it. Further, students can see that one of the triangles they create can be the result of a line reflection of the other, and the triangles are thus congruent.

Task 3.2

In figure 3.3, *EDB* is a line segment with $AD \cong CD$ and angle $ADE \cong$ angle CDE.

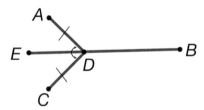

Fig. 3.3. Original figure

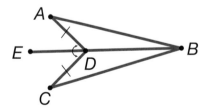

Fig. 3.4. Figure with line segments *AB* and *CB* drawn

(*a*) Draw line segments *AB* and *CB* to form triangles *ADB* and *CDB,* as in figure 3.4.

(*b*) List the new angles that have been formed.

(c) Make several conjectures about the new angles, line segments, and triangles that you have created. What can you conjecture about line segment *EB* in relation to angle *ABC?*

(d) Without measuring the angles or sides in the figure you drew, how can you determine whether your conjectures are true?

(e) Prove all the conjectures that you can.

A loosely scaffolded implementation of this problem could involve first eliciting all the conjectures from students. Then group students in pairs and assign each group to outline a plan to prove a particular conjecture. For example, two students outline a plan to prove AB ≅ *CB,* two students outline a plan to prove triangle *ADB* ≅ triangle *CDB,* and two students outline a plan to prove that EB is an angle bisector of angle ABC. After monitoring the students' work, select students to share the outlines of their plans, starting with the plan for proving the triangles congruent, to proving parts of the congruent triangles congruent, and finally, to proving the angle bisector plan. Various proofs can then be shared and analyzed by the class.

To provide more scaffolding for this problem, students could be prompted with such questions as the following:

- What questions should we ask about the pair of triangles that we created?

- What do we need to know about the triangles that would help us prove our conjectures?

- How could we prove this fact about the triangles?

- Once we prove this fact about the triangles, how does it help us? Why?

This series of questions allows teachers to preserve the "problem-solving" qualities of the activity by not spoon-feeding students what is needed, but by encouraging them to figure out what is needed for themselves. If, for example, we simply asked students to prove triangle *ADB* congruent to triangle *CDB,* the nature of the problem is fundamentally different.

Upon completion of this activity, students should be encouraged to reflect upon and revisit what they have accomplished. For example, they could be asked what they needed to establish in order to prove that *EB* is in fact an angle bisector.

STANDARDS *for Mathematical Practice—Tasks 3.1 and 3.2*

These congruence tasks reveal the essence of mathematical problem solving: Students work on making sense of the problem and its language, they explore relationships, they work backward to make a plan, they develop a proof, and they evaluate each other's work. In particular, students are asked not only to prove something, but also to determine what can be proved, and to figure out what questions can be asked and answered. They might use "guess and check," or examine cases in order to reach a conclusion for the problem.

They are also encouraged to reflect on the processes they have used and to organize and summarize their results. Four of the Standards for Mathematical Practice are supported in the congruence tasks (i.e., standards 1, 3, 4, and 5).

MP.1

By being asked to "analyze givens, constraints, relationships, and goals" and being required to determine what must be proven and what can be proven, students are "mak[ing] sense of problems and persever[ing] in solving them" (CCSSI 2010, p. 6). Task 3.2 not only develops mathematically proficient students by asking them to analyze goals, but also to determine what those goals should be, because *they* determine what can be proved. In this way this problem also supports development of mathematically proficient students who "make conjectures about the form and meaning of the solution and plan a solution pathway rather than simply jumping into a solution attempt" (CCSSI 2010, p. 6). The carefully structured parts of the question address this goal.

MP.3

By making conjectures with other students and testing and eventually proving them, students are becoming mathematically proficient as stated in MP.3, as they construct viable arguments and critique the reasoning of others. Specifically, students must "justify their conclusions, communicate them to others, and respond to the arguments of others" (CCSSI 2010, pp. 6–7) in order to complete task 3.2 successfully.

MP.4

In task 3.1 students can compare the diagram of the bridge shown in figure 3.1 to a picture of a "real" truss bridge, such as can be found on the web at *www.atlaso.com/bridge. htm.* This requires students to see the use of modeling mathematically to reach conclusions. They must use mathematics in order to reach further conclusions concerning a real-life situation.

MP.5

If a teacher elects to use dynamic geometry software to support students' completion of these tasks, MP.5, "Use appropriate tools strategically," is supported (CCSSI 2010, p. 7). Students must know the strengths and limitations of the software, and what conclusions may or may not be reasonably reached. In fact, these limitations often further support the need for proof.

Similarity

The topic of similarity is one of the most interesting in geometry, as its applications abound in our everyday lives. For example, as a launch question, students might be asked to consider what makes an enlarged picture look just like a small picture (see figs. 3.5 and 3.6). Task 3.3 provides an opportunity for students to examine the concepts of similar figures, addressing many of the standards and clusters of the domain of Similarity, Right

Triangles, and Trigonometry (G-SRT), particularly the cluster that includes standards G-SRT.1, G-SRT.2, and G-SRT.3, "Understand similarity in terms of similarity trans-formations" (CCSSI 2010, p. 77). Students will need rulers and protractors to examine lengths (e.g., arm of chair, top of head to ground) and angle measures (e.g., angles formed by parts of the chair, angle formed by the horizon and the vertical post). Rather than using the photo provided, teachers may decide to have students take their own photos, and then have them distort the photos using software. These can be projected using a computer or interactive whiteboard.

Task 3.3

(*a*) Examine the photographs in figures 3.5 and 3.6. What are the features of the picture that have stayed the same? What features have changed? Use a ruler and protractor to compare measures between the pictures.

Fig. 3.5. Original photo

Fig. 3.6. Enlarged photo

(*b*) What makes the photograph in figure 3.7 look distorted? What are the features that have changed? Stayed the same? Compare the distances from the top of the head to the armrest in all the pictures. Also compare the length of one of the posts in all three pictures. Compare the angle formed by the back leg of the chair and its shadow on the ground in all three pictures. What do you notice about the comparisons?

Fig. 3.7. Distorted photo

(*c*):

(i) Examine the three triangles in figure 3.8. Measure all three sides and all three angles of each triangle. Record your findings.

(ii) Make two observations about the measures you found. What is different about certain measures in the third triangle?

Fig. 3.8a. A triangle

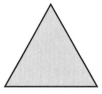

Fig. 3.8b. The triangle from figure 3.8a with all sides changed

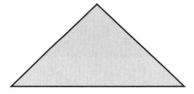

Fig. 3.8c. The triangle from figure 3.8a with the base changed further

After the exploratory activities above, teachers might elicit the definition of similar triangles from the students. Teachers might elect simply to share the images with students rather than have them work through the written questions, with the intention that students would gain an intuitive understanding of similarity, and how all lengths must be changed proportionally. Task 3.4, similar to that in Sultan and Artzt (2010, p. 369), can then be given to students in order to solidify the concepts regarding proportions in similar triangles, again addressing the standards of the G-SRT domain.

Task 3.4

(*a*) Using a ruler, a pen, and a piece of paper, draw a triangle. Label the vertices *A*, *B*, and *C*. Starting at vertex *A*, extend side *AB* by twice its own length to point *D*. (Segment *AD* will now be three times as long as segment *AB*.) Now, from vertex *A*, extend side *AC* by twice its own length to point *E*. (Segment *AE* will now be three times as long as segment *AC*.)

(*b*) Measure the lengths of side *AB*, segment *AD*, side *AC*, and segment *AE*.

(*c*) Measure the length of side *BC*. Based on what you have measured in part (*b*), what do you predict is the length of side *DE* of a triangle *ADE*? After your prediction, check by measuring side *DE*.

(*d*) What is the relationship between triangles *ABC* and *ADE*? Why do you believe this is true?

Students can glean many concepts involving similarity from this task. As designed, the students are considering the dilation of triangle *ABC* about center *A* with scale factor 3. In order to have a variety of triangles similar to triangle *ABC*, students might be given a variety of scale factors, including some less than one. Additionally, either of the other two vertices might be used as a center of dilation, which can lead to discussion about whether the triangles resulting from dilations about point *A* are similar to triangles resulting from a dilation about point *B* or *C*.

A further extension of this activity would allow students to examine the scale factor of the perimeter and area of the similar triangles. Students could cut out a duplicate of the smaller triangle and informally see how many smaller triangles would be needed to "cover" the larger triangle. For example, in the task as given, nine triangles that are the same size as triangle *ABC* are necessary to cover triangle *ADE*. Prior to investigating area and perimeter, students might be asked to make a conjecture about the ratios of the areas of similar triangles and the ratios of perimeters of similar triangles. Finally, this activity could also be done using graph paper, so there would be no need for rulers. But in many cases students would need to use the Pythagorean theorem in order to determine the length of some of the sides of the triangles. We believe that the task becomes more rich and meaningful if done in a cooperative work setting, allowing pairs or small groups of students to share ideas and conjectures, and requiring them to defend their thinking to their peers.

After completing these tasks, students should describe the relationships that exist among the lengths, the perimeters, the areas, and the angles of similar triangles. Given their conclusions, students should then explain why a person looks the same in a picture whether it is small or large.

STANDARDS *for Mathematical Practice—Tasks 3.3 and 3.4*

Tasks 3.3 and 3.4 support the development of mathematically proficient students by providing opportunities for students to make and test conjectures regarding similarity, communicate with their peers, and construct arguments to defend their ideas. A discussion of standards 2, 3, 4, and 7 of the Standards for Mathematical Practice follows.

MP.2

Completion of these tasks requires students to be able to work from the photograph and diagrams provided to create more abstract representations, working from both as appropriate. Students must "contextualize" and "decontextualize" as necessary in order to represent the problem at hand, thereby "reason[ing] abstractly and quantitatively" (CCSSI 2010, p. 6). They must realize that the measures with which they are working are related to an actual photograph but also be able to work with the out-of-context measures of parts of the photograph in order to examine the scale factor of the enlargements and the measures of the angles formed from corresponding parts of the photograph and diagram.

MP.3

In completing task 3.4, students must synthesize the information they have and the impact of extending two of the sides of the triangle, creating a similar triangle. They must make a reasonable conjecture about the length of the third side, and if the problem is extended, they must also make a conjecture about the relationship between areas and the perimeters of the two triangles, eventually "build[ing] a logical progression of statements to explore the truth of their conjectures," as described in the discussion of standard 3, "Construct viable arguments and critique the reasoning of others" (CCSSI 2010, p. 6). If, as suggested, teachers implement this activity in cooperative groups or pairs, students have the additional opportunity to "justify their conclusions, communicate them to others, and respond to the arguments of others" (CCSSI 2010, pp. 6–7).

MP.4

The "real-life" nature of the tasks and the requirement that students translate what they see in the photo and diagram require students to model mathematically, thereby addressing standard 4, "Model with mathematics." Students must "identify important quantities in a mathematical situation" and "analyze those relationships mathematically to draw conclusions" (CCSSI 2010, p. 7), specifically those regarding similarity.

MP.7

By using the drawings that they have created in task 3.4, either on plain paper or on graph paper, students must make use of the underlying mathematical structure of similarity, and the relationship to scale factor dilations about a vertex of the triangle in order to investigate the conjectures that they have made. Students have the opportunity to examine the creation of similar triangles using a variety of scale factors, and also using different vertices of the triangle as the center of the dilation. They should reach the conclusion that regardless of which vertex is used as the center, and what scale factor is used, every triangle created will be similar to the original triangle. Students must also make use of the structural aspects of the picture when examining the ratios of perimeters and the ratios of areas of any pair of similar triangles.

Expressing Geometric Properties with Equations

It is very exciting when connections can be made between two or more branches of mathematics. Interesting and unexpected connections can often be made. For example, if we place a circle, O, on a coordinate grid, we can find an equation that represents every point on the circumference of the circle, one based on a surprising connection to the Pythagorean theorem. By dropping a perpendicular from any point on a circle centered at the origin to the x-axis, the relationship between many interesting problems can be solved using this equation. Task 3.5 addresses the first cluster of the domain G-GPE: "Translate between the geometric description and the equation for a conic section" (CCSSI 2010, p. 78).

Task 3.5

Point A is plotted on the coordinate plane. The coordinates of point A are $(5, -6)$.

(a) What is an equation of the circle whose center is A that is tangent to the x-axis?

(b) What is an equation of the circle whose center is A that is tangent to the y-axis?

(c) What is an equation of the circle whose center is A that does not intersect either the x-axis or the y-axis?

(d) What is an equation of the circle whose center is A and intersects both the x- and y-axes?

(e) Find a range of values for the radii that satisfy the requirements of part (c).

(f) Find a range of values for the radii that satisfy the requirements of part (d).

(g) Find a range of values for the radii for a circle centered at A that intersect the x-axis in two points.

Working through this task allows students to think deeply about the structure of circles on the coordinate plane and the effect of particular constraints on the circle and its equations. Teachers may elect to add different constraints to the problem. For example, any center may be used, and students might each use a different center to allow for a variety of circles. Similarly, different lines can be used instead of the axes. For example, students might be asked to write an equation for a circle tangent to the line whose equation is $y = 2x$. Alternatively, students can be asked to write their own problems, creating different constraints and possibly sharing the problems with the rest of the class to solve. The nature of the problem might allow for students' working together cooperatively, encouraging communication among students. Additionally, dynamic geometry software could be used to investigate the circles that satisfy each constraint, and the equations of these circles.

In looking back on the solutions to the problem, students should be encouraged to think about the impact each constraint had on the solution, and which constraints allowed for a range of solutions as opposed to a single solution. Students should also be encouraged continually to check their work and the reasonableness of their solutions.

STANDARDS *for Mathematical Practice—Task 3.5*

Task 3.5 supports the development of mathematically proficient students by allowing students to examine a situation where they need to think about the entry points of the solution for each part of the problem and must persevere in solving the problem. Students must defend their solutions to the rest of the class, and to their cooperative group if teachers elect to use this teaching strategy. The nature of the problem requires that students use tools appropriately (i.e., this might be dynamic geometry software or simply pencil and graph paper) and use structure to reach a solution. A discussion of standards 1, 5, and 7 of the Standards for Mathematical Practice follows.

MP.1

As stated in CCSS: "Mathematically proficient students start by explaining to themselves the meaning of a problem and looking for entry points to its solution" (CCSSI, p. 6). Task 3.5 provides several constraints that must be analyzed in order to determine an appropriate solution. In examining the variety of constraints and the equations that satisfy them, students continually monitor their progress. In some cases there are many answers, and in others, only one circle will satisfy the constraints.

MP.5

In order to solve the problem satisfactorily, students must use appropriate tools strategically. A compass along with graph paper and pencil can allow students to explore the solutions that meet each constraint in the problem. Dynamic geometry software will also allow students to investigate solutions to each part of the problem, given each constraint.

MP.7

The underlying mathematical structure of circles, and the idea that two pieces of information, the center and radius, determine a circle are reinforced through this activity.

Students can investigate this structure by changing one or both of the center and radius, and then study the impact of each change on the resulting circle within the context of the coordinate plane.

Circles

A large part of the geometry curriculum involves the study of circles, their radii, their diameters, their circumferences, and their areas. In high school, students focus on the angles and their related intercepted arcs. Typically, students commit to memory the myriad of formulas representing these relationships, but they rarely have the opportunity to make conjectures about the relationships of the sizes of the different types of angles that intercept the same arcs. In tasks 3.6 and 3.7, students not only make these conjectures but are also led to discover ways they can verify and even prove them.

Task 3.6

Distribute to students "Exploring Angles in a Circle!" handouts containing three congruent circles, one with central angle *AOB* intercepting arc *AB* (see fig. 3.9a), another with inscribed angle *ACB* that intercepts the same arc *AB* (see fig. 3.9b), and a third with angle *ADB* that also intercepts arc *AB*, but where *D* is outside the circle and whose sides intercept the circle at points *E* and *F* (see fig. 3.9c). Note that to show students that the relationships hold regardless of the sizes of the circles and the measures of the intercepted arcs, multiple handouts can be distributed, each with different-size circles and measures of intercepted arcs (see figs. 3.9d–f).

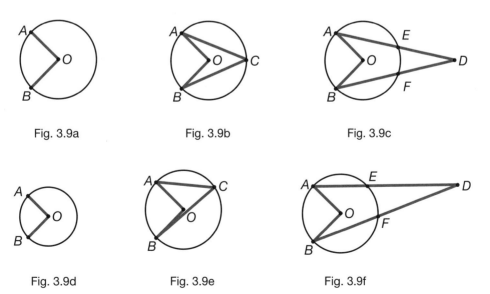

Fig. 3.9a   Fig. 3.9b   Fig. 3.9c

Fig. 3.9d   Fig. 3.9e   Fig. 3.9f

As a launch question, students are asked to make conjectures regarding the relative sizes of angle *AOB,* angle *ACB,* and angle *ADB.* For example, ask them whether they think that angle *ACB* is larger or smaller than angle *AOB,* and whether it is larger or smaller than angle *ADB.* Ask them to trace angle *ACB* and then lay their tracing onto angle *AOB* to see whether they can make a conjecture as to its specific relationship to angle *AOB.* It is hoped that students will come to notice that, given the same intercepted arc, the size of the angle decreases as the vertex of the angle is extended from the center of the circle to the circumference of the circle, and then outside the circle.

Having engaged in this initial exploration, students are now ready for task 3.7, which will lead them to discover more specific relationships.

Task 3.7

(*a*) Draw a circle with center *O,* and draw a central angle *AOB* that measures 60 degrees. (See fig. 3.9a for how the students' pictures should appear.)

(*b*) Pick a point *C* on major arc *AB* (see fig. 3.9b) and measure angle *ACB.* Pick a different point for *C* on major arc *AB* and again measure angle *ACB.* Do this one more time with yet a different point on major arc *AB.* What do you notice about your measurements?

(*c*) Pick a point *D* outside the circle and draw lines *DA* and *DB* (see fig. 3.9c). Measure arcs *EF* and *AB* that lie between *AD* and *BD,* and then measure angle *D.* Do this for two other locations of a point *D* outside the circle. Make a conjecture about how the measure of angle *D* is related to the measures of minor arcs *AB* and *EF.*

(*d*) Suppose you drew two chords in a circle, chord *AB* and chord *CD,* and they intersected at *E.* What would you guess is the relationship between the measure of angle *AEC* and the measures of arcs *AC* and *BD*? Verify your conjecture by measuring.

In completing task 3.7, students gain an intuitive sense of the relationships among the angles formed within a circle, and how the angle gets smaller as the vertex moves farther outside the circle. If teachers elect to do so, students can complete this task using dynamic geometry software. Further, students should be encouraged to prove their results. Teachers may decide to provide a recording sheet for students to organize and examine the measures of the angles with which they are working.

In completing this problem, students should be continually encouraged to look back on their conjectures, testing as they proceed to determine the correctness of their solutions and the verity of their conjectures.

STANDARDS *for Mathematical Practice—Tasks 3.6 and 3.7*

In order to complete this activity successfully, students must use appropriate tools, such as graph paper or dynamic geometry software. They gain informal insight into the relationships of the angles within the circle, allowing them to convince themselves that their conjecture makes sense before they prove it. As students examine the changes in the measures of the angles as they change, they discover the patterns that exist within the angles of a circle. A discussion of standards 5 and 8 of the Standards for Mathematical Practice follows.

MP.5

Students must use pencil, graph paper, and measurement tools successfully to determine the angle measures that are formed and the changes that take place within the problem. This task supports the development of mathematically proficient students by requiring that students know which tools to use and when each is appropriate.

MP.8

When formulating conjectures and examining the changes in angle measures within the circles in the activity, students must "look for and express regularity in repeated reasoning" (CCSSI 2010, p. 8). Particularly if using a recording sheet, students can examine the changes in the angles that are formed as the changes are made, finally generalizing and proving the result.

Chapter 4

Statistics and Probability

I n this age of information bombardment, it is hard to imagine that there was a time when concepts of statistics and probability were unknown. In fact, in comparison with many other popular branches of mathematics, the birth of statistics and probability occurred extremely late, not until the mid-seventeenth century. The word *probability* is derived from the verb meaning "probe," in the sense of testing or examining to find out something that is not easily accessible or understandable. As the word suggests, an informal definition of the word *probability* is the quality or condition of being probable. The word *statistics* is derived from the Italian word meaning "state," since the original concept of statistics was the collection of information about and for the government (Pickover 2009). Today, the study of statistics and probability is essential for an educated citizenry. In a digital age where information is being recorded at an astounding rate, people are seeking ways to capture and interpret data so that they can make decisions based on facts and not merely on intuitions. For this reason, it is important that students gain experience in examining real-life data that they can relate to and that they learn how these data can be organized, described, and interpreted in ways that will lead to probabilistic determinations.

In this chapter, we will use a problem-solving approach in which students can examine interesting data, ask questions about the data, and make predictions based on the data. We will explore different statistical methods students can use to examine their data, as well as probabilistic methods they can use to make their predictions. Through experimentation, students will also learn that a statement of probability will never tell you what *will* happen, but rather what is *likely* to happen.

Of the four domains of the high school standards for Statistics and Probability, the three required of all students are presented here. The eleven tasks in this chapter support these three domains:

- Interpreting Categorical and Quantitative Data—tasks 4.1 through 4.3
- Making Inferences and Justifying Conclusions—tasks 4.4 through 4.6
- Conditional Probability and the Rules of Probability—tasks 4.7 through 4.11

Along with the problems supporting each of these domains are suggestions for classroom implementation. The Standards for Mathematical Practice (MP) are woven throughout the three domains. Depending on the problem, the relevant standards (all of which are listed on page vi) are discussed specifically.

One of the exciting things about the mathematics curriculum is how the different branches of mathematics can be connected, resulting in a deeper conceptual understanding of all concepts involved. Although ideas such as linear regression, curve fitting, and graphing linear equations can be addressed in students' study of algebra or functions, they also have a place in the study of statistics and probability.

Interpreting Categorical and Quantitative Data

The tasks described below are meant to exemplify how powerful a problem-solving approach can be for examining statistical data, modeling it mathematically with appropriate tools, using algebraic reasoning to examine its structure, and then using that structure to make probabilistic determinations. Real data that will capture the interest of high school students can easily be found on the Internet. A good launch question might be to ask students what age they think they will live to, and why. After sharing their guesses and conjectures, the discussion can turn to whether they think they will be more or less likely to live to an older age than previous generations, and why. They can make conjectures to support their arguments that involve such issues as eating trends, the recent increase in obesity and other health-related issues, the current emphasis on exercise, expected advances in medicine, and other factors. The students can be encouraged to figure out how they might resolve the question of life-expectancy trends.

They may find information regarding different life expectancies by gender, race/ethnicity, and geographic location. Through the examination of the data, students can be encouraged to ask other questions regarding the general trends they notice. To get more information from the data, they will need to organize it and represent it in several ways, including graphically. Task 4.1 is designed to address several of the standards under the S-ID domain, including S-ID.6, "Represent data on two quantitative variables on a scatterplot and describe how the variables are related," and standards S-ID.7, 8, and 9 in the cluster "Interpret linear models" (CCSSI 2010, p. 81). For this task, the bivariate quantitative data in table 4.1 will be used. After observing the general trends in the data, students will represent the data visually by creating hand-drawn scatterplots on graph paper and then use their graphing calculators. With this new visual representation, new questions will arise. For example, students may now wonder how rapid the increase in life expectancy may be. Does it increase in a linear fashion? Exponentially? If it is linear, what is the rate of increase? Will the rate of increase continue forever? How might these questions be answered?

Task 4.1

Questions (*a*) through (*g*) refer to table 4.1.

(*a*) Plot the data points by hand on a coordinate plane. Consider carefully the values you use on the *x*-axis.

(*b*) What do you predict the life expectancy will be of a person born in 2020? 2050? Does this increase follow a linear relationship? An exponential relationship?

(*c*) Use a straightedge to create the line that you believe best fits the data. Why did you draw this line as you did?

(*d*) Use your knowledge of slope and *y*-intercept to write the equation of your line.

(*e*) Compare this line and its equation with other students' results. Are the lines the same or different? What do you think the qualities of a line of "best fit" should be?

(*f*) Enter the data into a graphing calculator and use the linear regression feature to determine the line of best fit. How does this line compare with your line?

(*g*) In addition to the slope and *y*-intercept, your calculator also shows an *r*-value. What do you think this *r*-value means?

Table 4.1
Average life expectancies of people born in a given year in the United States

Year	Life Expectancy
1920	54.1
1930	59.7
1940	62.9
1950	68.2
1960	69.7
1970	70.8
1980	73.7
1990	75.4
2000	77.0
2010	78.3

(*Compiled from:* http://www.infoplease.com/ipa/A0005148.html; http://www.census.gov/compendia/statab/2012/tables/12s0104.pdf; http://www.mikalac.com/tech/sta/long.html)

In part (*c*), it is likely that some students drew a line that went through the maximum number of points. Others might have drawn the line that divided the number of points somewhat equally on both sides. Comparing their result with that of the graphing calculator should spark discussion about the new value, the correlation coefficient, *r*. Students will probably notice that the equations they found and the one found by the calculator are somewhat different. By now, the students should be wondering how the calculator found the line of best fit, as well as what *r* means.

Meaningful discussions can ensue about the effects of using the years 1920 to 2010 versus using only the ten-year intervals 20 through 110 on the linear equations they calculate. Teachers should help their students to recognize that if they do not use the ten-year intervals and omit the "full years," they will get *y*-intercept values that will not make sense in terms of the problem. Calculating the line of best fit using the actual years will, of course, give a line with the same slope, but with a *y*-intercept of –430. What would this mean? Are we considering the year 0? What does an average life expectancy of –430 mean? Clearly, this does not make sense in the context of this problem. This is why we have subtracted 1900 from each year and used the ten-year intervals starting with 0 along the *x*-axis (see figs. 4.1 and 4.2).

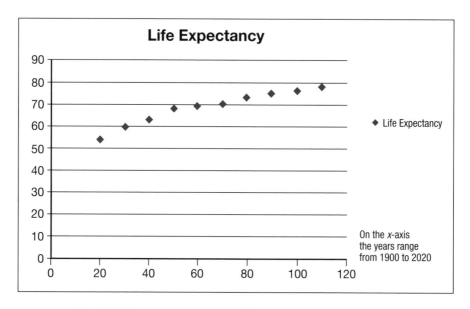

Fig. 4.1. Life expectancy scatterplot, data in ten-year intervals

At this point in the activity, students are confronted with figure 4.2, which contains the actual line of best fit, as well as the information provided by the calculator containing values for the slope, the *y*-intercept, and the mysterious value *r*. The first question to arise is how did the calculator find the line of best fit? What is the method that mathematicians have agreed on? In order to examine this question, students can explore the applet from NCTM Illuminations called "Linear Regression I," which allows them to investigate the behaviors of the regression line. This applet is available at http://illuminations.nctm.org /activitydetail.aspx?id=82. After this, they can use the e-Example 7.4 from the NCTM website, "Understanding the Least-Squares Regression Line with a Visual Model: Measuring Error in a Linear Model." This applet allows students to explore three methods for measuring how well a linear model fits a set of points: distance squared, absolute value, and shortest distance. This e-Example is available at http://www.nctm.org /standards/content.aspx?id=26787.

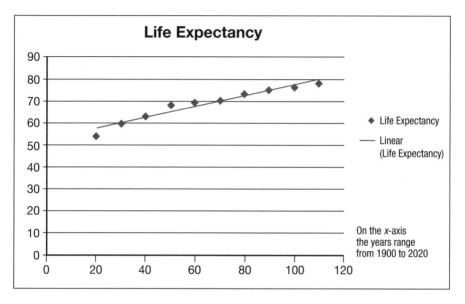

Fig. 4.2. Life expectancy scatterplot with the line of best fit

At the conclusion of this activity, students will learn that the line of best fit is defined to be the line with the property that the sum of the squares of the vertical distances of the *y*-coordinates of the data points from the line is a minimum, or as shown in the applet, the Least-Squares regression line. Students may still be uncomfortable with the fact that sometimes even the "official" line of best fit does not fit very well at all. An exploration such as the one below in task 4.2 will give them a feel for how the value of *r* is affected by different linear fits, thus addressing the standard S-ID.6, "Represent data on two quantitative variables on a scatterplot, and describe how the variables are related," and S-ID.8, "Compute . . . and interpret the correlation coefficient of a linear fit" (CCSSI 2010, p. 81). If preferred, this task may be completed using the applet mentioned above rather than a graphing calculator.

Task 4.2

Using a graphing calculator, do the following and record your answers.

(*a*) Enter points (1, 1), (2, 2), (3, 3), (4, 4). Find the line of best fit. How well did the line fit the points? What is the value of *r*?

(*b*) Enter points (–1, 1), (–2, 2), (–3, 3), (–4, 4). Find the line of best fit. How well did the line fit the points? What is the value of *r*?

(*c*) Enter the points (1, 3), (2, 2), (3, 5), (4, 2). Find the line of best fit. How well did the line fit the points? What is the value of *r*?

(*d*) Enter the points (1, 0) (2, 2), (3, 5), (4, 6). Find the line of best fit. How well did the line fit the points? What is the value of *r*?

(*e*) Enter the points (1, 2), (1, 8), (6, 2), (6, 8). Find the line of best fit. How well did the line fit the points? What is the value of *r*?

(*f*) What conjectures can you make about the range of *r*-values and how it varies with the goodness of fit of a line?

(*g*) In our problem regarding life expectancy, what was the *r*-value? How good was the fit?

In task 4.2, students develop an understanding of the relationship of the *r*-value to the linear relationship of the data points. An extension of this problem might be to ask students to create their own sets of points that fit given criteria for *r*. For example, students could be asked to create a set of four points (different from above) that have a "strong" positive correlation.

As we recall, this exploration began with the question about whether the students would have a greater life expectancy than generations past. Because this is a futuristic question, no data beyond what we have about the past and the present are available. Now students need to consider the predictive value of the lines they found, along with the meaning of the slope and *y*-intercept for their models. In this particular case, the *r*-value is 0.97, which is quite high, indicating a strong linear correlation among the data. The slope is *a* = 0.2539, and the *y*-intercept is 52.47. Below are important questions for students to consider, some of which get at the heart of probabilistic concepts and misconceptions. Task 4.3 addresses many standards in the S-ID domain, including S-ID.6, 7, and 8. Further, many of the standards for functions are met by this rich task, including F-IF.4 and 5; F-BF.1a; and F-LE.2.

Task 4.3

These questions should be answered based on the line of best fit you determined in task 4.1.

   (*a*) According to your line of best fit, what do you predict your life expectancy will be?

   (*b*) Does this mean that you will live to that exact age? Explain.

   (*c*) According to your line of best fit, what will the average life expectancy be in the year 2050? In the year 2100? 3000? 4000?

   (*d*) According to your line of best fit, will there be a time when people live until 1,000? Explain.

   (*e*) Discuss the benefits and limitations of the predictive values of lines of best fit.

   (*f*) Explain what the slope and *y*-intercept values mean for the linear model.

In considering the questions above, students should realize that life expectancy cannot increase indefinitely, and that expectancies larger than, say, 120, are probably unrealistic. In examining the slope and *y*-intercept in part (*f*), students should be able to explain that the minimum life expectancy *according to our model* is 52.47, and that the slope of 0.2539 indicates that for every year later one is born, life expectancy increases by 0.2539 years.

Functions serve as excellent models in all areas of life to help us determine how certain things relate to each other. In fact, they often explain laws of nature and the behaviors of natural phenomena. Their predictive value ranges from making weather forecasts to determining insurance rates for car drivers. But, as with all probabilistic statements, a prediction is just that—it can never tell us exactly what *will* happen; it can tell us only what is *likely* to happen. And in some cases, if the function values go beyond a certain point, there can be *no* predictive value.

STANDARDS *for Mathematical Practice—Tasks 4.1 through 4.3*

The rich tasks above create opportunities to meet several of the Standards for Mathematical Practice for mathematically proficient students through problem solving (i.e., standards 2, 4, and 5). By making and testing predictions and conjectures and analyzing their results, students are "building new mathematical knowledge through problem solving" (NCTM 2000, p. 334). Students have the opportunity to examine the power and limitations of statistical models, and to consider the reasonableness of their responses.

MP.2

When determining the usefulness of the model, and for what values the model has meaning, students are "reason[ing] abstractly and quantitatively" (CCSSI 2010, p. 6). For example, in the year 2250, the x-value that is consistent with our model is 350, with a corresponding y-value of 141.335, indicating a life expectancy of more than 141 years. Students can discuss whether or not this prediction is reasonable within the context of the problem.

MP.4

Tasks 4.1 and 4.3 ask students to create a mathematical model for prediction that can be used to extend the model beyond the known data points. At the same time, students must realize when the model is no longer useful, such as when predicted life expectancy surpasses a level that no longer seems reasonable for a human life expectancy. Students must also make sense out of the slope and y-intercept, explaining for every "change in x" by 1 (year born) that the "change in y" increases by 0.2539 years (life expectancy). The y-intercept indicates the initial value of life expectancy for the model (in this case, the average life expectancy in the year 1900).

MP.5

Students are required to use a variety of tools in this series of problems, from simple tools such as graph paper and straightedge to graphing calculators and online applets. Task 4.2 allows students to use an applet to make conclusions about the meaning of r, which is the correlation coefficient, and what it tells us about the strength of the linear relationship. Although it is not always practical for students to use a straightedge to calculate the line of best fit by hand, it can be a worthwhile exercise. It can reveal to the teacher some common misconceptions about the "best" line, such as that the best line needs to intersect many data points.

Making Inferences and Justifying Conclusions

When students think of probability, the first thing that comes to their minds might be rolling dice or tossing a coin. Rarely do they think of the probabilistic decisions they make on a daily basis. Consider a day in the life of a high school student headed for school in the morning. What are the chances my team will win today? What is the weather forecast? How likely is it that it will snow today? How likely is it that the bus will arrive on time? What are the chances that the bus will have an accident if it does snow? How are these things determined? Little do high school students realize that the answers to all these questions can be determined from probabilistic calculations based on vast amounts of data collected over long periods of time—in other words, experimental probability. The tasks in this section demonstrate how teachers can bridge the gap between students' understanding of theoretical and experimental probability and can deepen their often naïve and mistaken understanding of these concepts and how they actually play a role in their daily lives.

The intention of task 4.4 is to target common probabilistic misconceptions that students often have, including the "gambler's fallacy." These concepts often seem counterintuitive to students and adults alike. Task 4.4 addresses standard S-IC.2, "Decide if a specified model is consistent with results from a given data-generating process," and S-IC.3, "Recognize the purposes of and differences among sample surveys, experiments, and observational studies" (CCSSI 2010, p. 81).

Task 4.4

Ask students to comment on the following:

Mary has tossed a coin twenty times and has arrived at the following outcome: HHHHHTTTTTTTTTTTTTTT (i.e., five heads followed by fifteen tails). Critique the comments made by the following students:

(*a*) Joshua says that the coin is not fair since an equal number of heads and tails should have been tossed—that is, ten heads and ten tails.

(*b*) Sarah says that Mary was not tossing the coin correctly since the outcomes should have occurred in a more random order—that is, not all the heads together followed by all the tails together.

(*c*) Caleb says that if Mary had tossed twenty different coins, one after the other, there is no way it could have come out with five heads followed by fifteen tails.

(*d*) Olivia says that she is really certain that if Mary tossed the coin again a head would come up, since there had already been such a long string of tails.

After students have considered each of these situations on their own, they can be asked to discuss them with their peers or group members. Critical and yet very common misconceptions underlie the comments made by the four fictional students:

1. Joshua assumes that a small number of tosses will necessarily resemble the experimental probability that is estimated for an extremely large number of tosses.

2. Sarah thinks that randomness implies that a result must appear "haphazard" and cannot look very organized or orderly.

3. Caleb believes that the models of tossing one coin twenty times and tossing twenty different coins once are not equivalent for the purposes of this experiment.

4. Olivia holds that the previous outcomes can affect the likelihood of the current toss finally ending in a result that is "due." In her view, each toss of a coin is not in fact an independent event that is unaffected by previous occurrences.

Students learn a theoretical approach to probability that says that if an experiment can result in *n* equally likely outcomes, and if *E* is an event that occurs in precisely *m* out of the *n* outcomes, then the probability of that event occurring is *m/n*. In the case of the coin toss, there are two equally likely outcomes and tossing a head can happen in only one way. Also, tossing a tail can happen in only one way. Therefore, the probability that a head will appear on the toss of a fair coin is ½, and the same is true for the probability that a tail will appear.

But now a bigger question arises. Is there such an object as a fair coin? Every coin we use might have some weighting issues that make it more likely for one side to land over another. Nevertheless, we do use real coins as models of our theoretical concept of a "fair coin." And in fact, this model is used for some very important decisions. Just picture a tennis match where a flip of the coin is used to determine who serves first. With a model, we make use of an experimental or frequency approach to probability. For example, when we say that the probability of getting a head on the toss of a coin is ½, we are using a model that we believe suggests that many, many tosses will result in a proportion of heads that is about ½. We believe this since this particular model has been used for hundreds of years and has behaved in a way that is consistent with our suspicions that after a large number of flips, the proportion of heads is very close to ½.

Much of the school curriculum involves students in applying the classical approach to probability problems. Of course, the real-life examples referred to above are all dependent on an experimental or frequency approach. As entry into that way of thinking, it is often interesting and helpful for students to gain experience using a model for which there is no way of calculating a theoretical probability. Consider task 4.5, in which students are asked to consider, among other things, the tossing of a paper cup, for which there is no theoretical probability for the likelihood of how the cup will land. Will it land on its side? Right side up? Upside down? Task 4.5 further develops the concepts necessary to meet standards S-IC.2 and S-IC.3.

Task 4.5

Ask the students the following questions:

(*a*) If I were to toss a fair six-sided die once, would you expect that it would land on a side with exactly one dot? Why or why not?

(*b*) If I were to flip a coin once, would you expect that it would land on the side with a head? Why or why not?

(*c*) If I were to toss a paper cup, would you expect that it would land on its side? Why or why not?

As a result of this discussion, students might determine that in the first two examples the theoretical probabilities were known entities, that is, ⅙ and ½, respectively. They might discuss that they could be reasonably sure that the cup would land on its side, but they really did not know what the probability of landing on the side would be. Teachers can initiate discussion that would help students arrive at both the need for and method of determining an experimental probability for the cup toss. Interesting questions could arise during this discussion that would highlight the essential characteristics of the theoretical probabilities that apply to the die and the coin. For example, the teacher could elicit that there were, in fact, three ways that the cup could land—on its side, right side up, or upside down. Students might question whether this would mean that the probability of landing in any one of those ways would be ⅓, since there were three possible ways the cup could land—something that is not the case, even though there are three possible outcomes. In addition to meeting the standards met by task 4.5, task 4.6 also addresses standard S-ID.5, as cumulative relative frequencies are summarized using a table. Students should work in pairs for this activity.

Task 4.6

(a) Each pair of students tosses the cup up and lets it land twenty times, with one student tossing and the other student recording the results on a chart.

(b) Each pair enters their results on a class chart with cumulative proportions (# upside down/# of tosses, # right side up/# of tosses, # sideways/# of tosses) reported as each pair enters data.

(c) After examining the results, students consider the following questions: Would you expect that the cup would land on its side? After how many tosses would you be willing to decide? Why?

After concluding task 4.6, students should gain an understanding that experimental probability is sometimes the *only* means of calculating a probability, and that only after many, many, cases can any probabilistic determination or prediction be made. This experience provides a nice segue into how experimental probability is often the only way that a probability can be calculated in real-life situations. Some examples of such situations include probabilities for weather phenomena, natural disasters, car and other accidents, birthrates, and death rates. For example, students may wonder who pays more insurance for driving, women or men? The following probabilistic statement was made on the website of Car Accident Attorneys: "Men are more than twice as likely to die in a car crash than women." This statement is based on the car crash statistics given in table 4.2, showing that 73 percent of all people killed in car accidents are male. Students should be able to discuss whether or not the previous statement about the likelihood of dying in an accident is a valid conclusion, particularly because the data indicate only whether a driver was killed.

Table 4.2
Car crash data

Persons Killed, by Sex in the United States, 2006	
Male Drivers Killed	Female Drivers Killed
29,722	12,747
Total Both Sexes: 42,469	
(173 drivers of unknown sex not included)	

(*Source:* http://www.car-accidents.com/pages/car-crash-men-woman.html)

Other ways to extend this concept is to engage students in finding real-life data that lead to probabilistic determinations. Students might be asked (or might come up with their own questions) such as the following: Why is it recommended that people do not smoke? Why is obesity discouraged? Why should people wear seatbelts when driving in a car? Why shouldn't people text while driving? Using the Internet, they can find data that will help them answer the question. They can then use the data they have found to help give a probabilistic answer to the original question.

STANDARDS *for Mathematical Practice—Tasks 4.4 through 4.6*

The above problems facilitate students' meeting several of the Standards for Mathematical Practice through problem solving (i.e., standards 3, 4, and 5). Students must understand the problems at hand, and they must make a plan for what their approach to the problems will be. By checking their work and examining whether or not their responses are sensible, students gain a better understanding of the meaning of probability, and the notions of experimental and theoretical probabilities.

MP.3

In working with probabilistic situations that often defy intuition, students must rely on mathematical reasoning, and they need to be able to explain the important aspects of the experiment and the situation in order to solve the problems correctly. In task 4.4, students are presented with several common probabilistic misconceptions presented as statements of fictional students. Students must discuss the reasonableness of the statements and make reasonable arguments for why they do or do not agree with them, thus "construct[ing] viable arguments and critiqu[ing] the reasoning of others" (CCSSI 2010, p. 6). For example, students should be able to communicate that although it is counterintuitive, the outcome of the toss of a coin is not affected by prior coin tosses.

MP.4

In determining the experimental probability for the event in task 4.6, students are "model[ing] with mathematics," relating the experimental results determined from the real data generated by the students to experimental probabilities based on those results (CCSSI 2010, p. 7). Real data are organized in table form, allowing for a determination of probability. Through these tasks, students have the opportunity to see that many of the everyday probabilities they hear on a regular basis, such as the chance of rain, are based on models of experimental probability.

MP.5

Students, through tossing coins and conducting experiments using such nontraditional items as a paper cup, are "us[ing] appropriate tools strategically" (CCSSI 2010, p. 7). These tools allow students to base their understanding of probability on concrete examples, leading to a deeper understanding of experimental versus theoretical probability.

Conditional Probability and the Rules of Probability

A classic problem in probability, the "Birthday Problem," dates back to 1939 and is attributed to mathematician Richard von Mises (Jones 2012; von Mises 1964). One reason it is so well known is that its results are very counterintuitive. Although the numbers involved in analyzing the problem are rather large, the teacher can use a problem-solving approach of reducing it to a simpler problem as a means of giving students a better understanding of the original problem. This approach will be used in task 4.7.

Task 4.7

If we combined the students in our class with the students in the two math classes down the hall (a total of about sixty students), how certain could you be that at least two people out of all three classes would have the same birthday?

Before engaging in the activity, the students should have a chance to make guesses about what will happen. Most likely the students will think that because a year has 365 days (not counting leap year), there would have to be 366 people in order to be completely certain that at least two people in the group have the same birthday. Given this way of thinking, the students might be asked how many people do they think there would need to be in a group for there to be a 50 percent chance that at least two people have the same birthday. Students will likely guess that it is one half of 366, or about 183. They will be very surprised when they learn that there need be only twenty-three in a group to be about 50 percent sure there will be a match.

In preparation for this task, the teacher might ask each student in each of the three classes to write his or her birthday on a piece of paper. The teacher can then have each student in the class call out his or her birthday. If there is no match within the class, then the birthdays on the papers from the other two classes can be read aloud until a match is found. (A record should be kept of the number of birthdays it takes before a match is found.) Most surely, a match will be found, as there is over a 99 percent probability of a match with only sixty people.

At this point, the students should be questioning their original assumption that it would take 366 people in a group to guarantee a match. They will probably be wondering what the probability is of finding a match, given a certain number of people. It is at this point that the teacher should suggest that in order to analyze the problem, they might reduce it to a simpler one. By using the multiplication principle, permutations, and fundamental laws of probability they will be able to solve a seemingly complex and interesting problem.

In task 4.8, we are going to figure out the probability of three students chosen at random having the same birthday. Instead of considering the case where there are a large number of students being counted, we will begin with only three people and then generalize to a larger group.

Task 4.8

(a) If we choose three dates (representing three birthdays) at random, and list them in order, using the multiplication principle, how many ways can this be done? [$365 \times 365 \times 365$, or 365^3]

(b) If we choose three dates at random, and list them in order, using the multiplication principle, how many ways can this be done so that three *different* dates are chosen (that is, three different birthdays)? [$365 \times 364 \times 363$]

(c) What is the probability that the three dates chosen at random will be different (three different birthdays)?
[Use the definition of probability—that is, *P(Event) = Number of successes/ Number of ways the event can occur*—to elicit ($365 \times 364 \times 363$) / 365^3]

(d) What is the complement of the probability in part (c)? What does this tell us?
[$1 - (365 \times 364 \times 363) / 365^3$]

(e) Use your calculator to figure out the value of the probability in part (d). What is the likelihood that out of three people, at least two of them will share the same birthday? [0.008, very low]

(f) Do the calculation for five people and then for ten people, recording your results. How many people do you think you would have to have to be more than 50 percent sure that at least two of them have the same birthday?

(g) Examine the data in table 4.3, and discuss the results. Given what you know now, how certain would you be that in a group of sixty students at least two of them have the same birthday? Explain.

Table 4.3
Birthday problem data

People	Unique Days	Probability None the Same	Probability at Least Two the Same
1	365	1	0
2	364	0.997	0.003
3	363	0.992	0.008
4	362	0.984	0.016
5	361	0.973	0.027
6	360	0.960	0.040
7	359	0.944	0.056
8	358	0.926	0.074
9	357	0.905	0.095
10	356	0.883	0.117
11	355	0.859	0.141
12	354	0.833	0.167
13	353	0.806	0.194
14	352	0.777	0.223
15	351	0.747	0.253
16	350	0.716	0.283
17	349	0.685	0.315
18	348	0.653	0.347
19	347	0.621	0.379
20	346	0.589	0.411

Table 4.3—*Continued*

People	Unique Days	Probability None the Same	Probability at Least Two the Same
21	345	0.556	0.444
22	344	0.524	0.476
23	343	0.493	0.507
24	342	0.462	0.538
25	341	0.431	0.569
26	340	0.402	0.598
27	339	0.373	0.627
28	338	0.346	0.654
29	337	0.319	0.681
30	336	0.294	0.706
31	335	0.270	0.730
32	334	0.247	0.753
33	333	0.225	0.775
34	332	0.205	0.795
35	331	0.186	0.814
40	326	0.109	0.891
50	316	0.030	0.970
60	306	0.006	0.994

(*Source:* http://www1.appstate.edu/~kms/classes/psy2510/birthtable.html)

Note that with part (*f*) above, teachers could assign different numbers to different students (or pairs of students if they are working together) so that the work is not repetitive. Students can work cooperatively in order to calculate the probability for numbers other than five and ten. Teachers may choose the numbers they would like students to use, or allow students to choose their own number.

A common misconception associated with the "Birthday Problem" needs to be examined with students, and it is addressed in task 4.9.

Task 4.9

Several years ago, a popular talk show host was trying to demonstrate the surprising phenomena we just revealed in the "Birthday Problem." Not believing it could be true, he noted that there were about 120 people in his audience and asked how many of them shared his birthday, say, August 14. Much to his shock, none of them did.

Given the discoveries we have made above, discuss how you would have explained this situation.

(*a*) What is different about the problem the talk show host posed and the one posed in the birthday problem?

(*b*) What is the probability that if someone is chosen at random, that person's birthday is *not* August 14? [364/365]

(*c*) What is the probability that two people chosen at random do *not* have birthdays of August 14? [364/365 × 364/365]

(*d*) What is the probability that 120 people chosen at random do *not* have birthdays of August 14? [$(364/365)^{120}$, which is about 0.71949]

(*e*) Was the result the talk show host encountered surprising? Why or why not?

By contrasting the two problems above, teachers can engage their students in a discussion of how people underestimate the frequency of coincidences, and how they are so surprised when they occur. The "Birthday Problem" demonstrates how likely coincidence is. However, this cannot be confused by how much less likely it is for a specific occurrence to occur, such as is demonstrated in the talk show host problem (Paulos 1988).

Without realizing it, students are confronted with statements involving conditional probability on a daily basis. For example, they are told that if they are obese they have a greater risk of getting diabetes, or if they smoke they have a greater risk of getting lung cancer, or if they talk on the telephone or text while driving, they have a greater risk of getting into an accident. While most of these statements almost seem obvious today, they really are statements of conditional probability. We will examine this toward the end of the section, and we will continue here with a rather simple hands-on task that students should enjoy and that would lead them to the formal definition of conditional probability.

In task 4.10, we examine two events, *A* and *B*, and as a way of clarifying what conditional probability means we juxtapose $P(A \cap B)$ with $P(B|A)$. We do this first with a hands-on experiment, in an effort to help students get an understanding of the situation and begin to form conjectures about the relationship between the two probabilities; we then follow with a more abstract discussion. This task can be conducted in small groups, with pairs or triples of students enacting the experiment, or as a large group with a student at the board recording the outcomes and different students coming to the front of the room to enact each trial of the experiment. However it is done, thirty trials of each experiment should take place. This task addresses the standards in the S-CP domain of the CCSS.

Task 4.10

Consider a paper bag that has nine sourball candies, five of which are cherry and four of which are lemon.

(*a*) Shake up the bag to mix the candies and then, without looking, pick two candies out of the bag, one after the other. Record your answer in order. Return the candies to the bag and repeat the experiment twenty times, recording the results of each trial.

(*b*) How many times was a cherry candy picked first and a lemon candy second? Was it more or less than ten times (half the number of trials)? Does picking a cherry followed by a lemon seem to be a likely occurrence? Would you expect it to be? Why or why not?

(*c*) Now adjust the experiment by first removing a cherry candy from the bag and putting it to the side, simulating the occurrence that a cherry candy has been picked first. (Keep the cherry candy out for the whole experiment.) Now choose *one* candy and record the results. Repeat the experiment for a total of twenty trials, recording each outcome.

(*d*) Count the number of times a lemon candy was picked. Was it more or less than ten times (half the number of trials)? Does picking a lemon candy given that a cherry has already been picked seem to be a likely occurrence? Would you expect it to be? Why or why not? Would you expect it to be more likely than the event in example (*a*)?

(*e*) Explain in words what your conjecture is about the probabilities in examples (*a*) and (*c*) above.

Careful questioning about the experiments in task 4.10 will help teachers to elicit that $P(C \cap L)$ is less than $P(L|C)$. While it is true that given any particular experiment, anything can happen, having students engage in this task at least gives them a clearer understanding of the differences between the two scenarios that modeled the probability of two events happening versus conditional probability. It is hoped that the students will have some intuitions that $P(C \cap L)$ is less than $P(L|C)$.

Task 4.11 is an abstract model of the previous example that will lead to the formal definition of conditional probability. Students should work alone on the following questions. After a few minutes, have them confer with their partners or group mates.

Task 4.11

In our prior experiment we began with a paper bag that had nine sourball candies, five of which were cherry and four of which were lemon. Given that same scenario:

(a) Determine the probability of picking a cherry candy first and a lemon candy second.

(b) Determine the probability of picking a cherry candy out of the bag on the first pick.

(c) Determine the probability of picking a lemon candy given that a cherry candy had already been picked.

Given students' prior understanding of probability, they should be able to answer questions (a)–(c) correctly. Part (a) is $P(C \cap L) = \frac{5}{9} \times \frac{4}{8}$; part (b) is $P(C) = \frac{5}{9}$, while part (c) is $P(L|C) = \frac{4}{8}$. Question (a) is usually presented as a problem where you pick "without replacement" and students learn to multiply the probabilities of the events. But why are they multiplied? Since a first candy can be selected in nine ways and a second candy in eight ways, by the multiplication principle there are a total of 9×8 or 72 ordered pairs (candy 1, candy 2). If the first candy is to be cherry and the second to be lemon, then the first cherry candy can be chosen from any of the five cherry candies and the second, lemon candy can be chosen from any of the four lemon candies. Thus, there are 5×4 or 20 possibilities for the event $C \cap L$ to occur. As a result, the probability of getting a cherry candy on the first pick followed by a lemon candy on the second pick is $(5 \times 4)/(9 \times 8) = 20/72 = 5/18$ or about 28 percent.

Now how does this bring us to the definition of, or formula for conditional probability? Observe from questions (a), (b), and (c) that $P(C \cap L) = P(C) \times P(L|C)$. The fact is that this relationship is always true, and it is used to define conditional probability. That is, dividing both sides by $P(C)$, $P(L|C)$ is defined to be $P(C \cap L) / P(C)$, assuming that $P(C)$ is not zero. In the given problem, one might ask why the formula is even necessary, since to find $P(L|C)$ all we had to do was use a reduced sample space (since one candy had already been picked, there were eight instead of nine) to get $\frac{4}{8}$. The fact is that, in many problems, reducing the sample space is an excellent way of figuring out the probability.

STANDARDS *for Mathematical Practice—Tasks 4.7 through 4.11*

To solve the above problems successfully, problem-solving strategies must be employed. Students must make sure they understand the given problems, and they need to examine related simpler problems that allow them to make sense of the more complicated problems. New concepts are introduced through the carefully selected problems. Standards 2, 4, and 8 of the Standards for Mathematical Practice are supported by tasks 4.7 through 4.11.

MP.2

While carrying out the experiments that allow students to discover the relationships of conditional probability and the probability of dependent events, students must collect and analyze data and then compare the results for different conditions. This requires students to "reason abstractly and quantitatively" (CCSSI 2010, p. 6). Students must be mindful of the meaning of each of the experiments, and how they differ, in order to be able to reach and discuss meaningful conclusions about probability.

MP.4

In determining the experimental probability for the event in these tasks, students are "model[ing] with mathematics," again relating the experimental results determined from the real data generated by the students to experimental probabilities based on those results (CCSSI 2010, p. 7). Real data are organized in table form, allowing for the determination of conditional and dependent probabilities. The "Birthday Problem" models a situation that is very common and yet is quite counterintuitive. Students, as they work through the carefully sequenced questions, come to a surprising result about the likelihood of at least two people in a group sharing a birthday.

MP.8

Through examining the probabilities determined by the experiment in tasks 4.7 and 4.8, students must "look for and express regularity in repeated reasoning" (CCSSI 2010, p. 8). Students should examine the patterns and results in the outcomes that allow them to determine the general way of calculating the probabilities of conditional, dependent, and independent events.

Chapter 5

Number and Quantity

Mathematical historians have noted that the first number systems were analogous to the natural, or counting, numbers. As new needs arose, the systems of integers, rational, irrational, and complex numbers were developed. For example, it was only when humans realized they needed to represent zero and numbers less than zero that the natural numbers were expanded to include the concepts of zero and of negative numbers. When whole numbers needed to be divided into equal parts, the rational numbers were born. While studying right triangles and the Pythagorean theorem, people realized that the square root of 2 was incommensurate with the unit length, and this eventually led to the definition and development of irrational numbers. Finally, the search for solutions to quadratic equations and cubic equations led to the need to define the square root of –1, and with it the development of the imaginary numbers and the complex number system.

The Common Core State Standards have four domains for number and quantity; in this chapter we will present the three domains that are required of all students. The seven tasks given here support the following domains: (1) the Real Number System (tasks 5.1, 5.2, and 5.3); (2) Quantities (tasks 5.4 and 5.5); and (3) the Complex Number System (tasks 5.6 and 5.7). Along with the problems supporting each of these domains, we provide suggestions for classroom implementation. The Standards for Mathematical Practice (MP) are woven throughout the three domains, and for each problem we discuss the most relevant standards.

The Real Number System

In the middle grades, students learn the meaning of positive exponents and the rules of exponents, eventually extending their understanding to zero exponents and negative exponents. These rules can be developed by observing patterns in lists of exponents. For example, in examining the list $3^4 = 81$, $3^3 = 27$, $3^2 = 9$, and $3^1 = 3$, students can use the list's patterns to determine what 3^0, 3^{-1}, and 3^{-2} should be equal to if the pattern continues. Task 5.1 addresses the two standards under the domain N-RN, the Real Number System, that are within the cluster "Extend the properties of exponents to rational exponents" (CCSSI 2010, p. 60). The task is intended to build on students' prior knowledge of exponents to allow them to discover the meaning of fractional exponents. Before introducing task 5.1, it might be useful for teachers to ask students, "What does x^2 mean?" "What does x^3 mean?" and "Make a conjecture about what $x^{1/2}$ means."

Task 5.1

Express each in simplest form using exponents.

  (a) $x^3 \cdot x^3$

  (b) $x^2 \cdot x^2$

  (c) $x \cdot x$

  (d) $x^{1/2} \cdot x^{1/2}$

  (e) $x^{1/3} \cdot x^{1/3} \cdot x^{1/3}$

  (f) $x^{1/4} \cdot x^{1/4} \cdot x^{1/4} \cdot x^{1/4}$

  (g) In part (d), you got an answer of x. What quantity do you know of which when multiplied by itself gives x? Based on your answer, what do you think $x^{1/2}$ means? What do you think $x^{1/3}$ means? Why? What do you think $x^{1/4}$ means? Why?

The intention of part (g) is to relate the radical symbol to rational exponents. An extension of the task would be to ask students what they think $x^{3/4}$ means. Teachers should elicit from students that this is the same as $x^{1/4}$ cubed, the fourth root of x cubed, or x^3 raised to the ¼, so it is also the fourth root of x cubed. Students should also be asked to consider how they might write $\left(\sqrt{5}\right)^7$ so that they might practice "moving" back and forth between fractional exponents and radicals.

Task 5.2 provides questions that might be used as a launch for a lesson. This task is designed to correct common misconceptions about rational and irrational numbers, addressing standard N-RN.3, "Use properties of rational and irrational numbers" (CCSSI 2010, p. 60).

Task 5.2

  (a) Susie says 0.12112111211112... is rational because she can figure out what comes next. Do you agree with Susie? Why or why not? Is 0.12112111211112 rational?

  (b) Matt says that 2π is rational because the 2 is rational, and because $\pi = 3.14$. Do you agree with Matt? Why or why not?

Part (a) of task 5.2 targets the misconception that a decimal numeral is rational simply because there is a pattern to its digits, and it is thus predictable. Teachers should emphasize that "predictable" is not the same as "repeating," and that even if we can determine the next digits of a decimal expansion, the decimal is not rational unless it repeats. It is also important to discuss that the terminating decimal 0.12112111211112 is rational simply because it terminates. Part (*b*) addresses two common misconceptions. Students often forget that 3.14 is a rational approximation of π, and that π does not equal 3.14. Second, students often erroneously believe that because one of the numbers forming a product is rational, then the product must therefore be rational.

These ideas are further developed through task 5.3. Students are asked to examine different pairs of rational and irrational numbers, and determine whether the results of each sum or product are rational or irrational. This task builds on students' prior knowledge of rational and irrational numbers. Students examine whether, in general, the sums of pairs of rational and irrational numbers are themselves rational or irrational. This task further develops the concepts required to meet standard N-RN.3.

Task 5.3

I. Compute each sum or product and determine whether each is rational or irrational. Explain your reasoning:

(*a*) $0.12112111211112\ldots \bullet 2$

(*b*) $0.12112111211112\ldots + 0.21221222122221\ldots$

(*c*) $3 \bullet \sqrt{2}$

(*d*) $3 + \sqrt{2}$

(*e*) $\sqrt{3} \bullet \sqrt{3}$

(*f*) $\pi \bullet 2$

(*g*) $-\pi + \pi$

(*h*) $\frac{2}{9} + \frac{5}{17}$

II. Based on parts (*a*) through (*h*) above, determine whether each of the following is true:

i.   The sum of two rational numbers is always rational.

ii. The sum of two irrational numbers is always irrational.

iii. The sum of an irrational number and a rational number is irrational.

iv. The product of two rational numbers is always rational.

v.   The product of two irrational numbers is always irrational.

vi. The product of an irrational number and a rational number is irrational.

The six questions in part II provide an opportunity to discuss informally the proofs of each of these cases. The proofs of (i) and (iv) rely on the properties of the rational numbers and can be proved directly. When considering (iii) and (vi) we must consider an indirect proof. That is, if we want to prove that the sum of an irrational number and a rational number is always irrational, we must first assume that some number q is rational and some number x is irrational (not = 0), but if their product R is rational, then we get a contradiction. If $qx = R$, then $x = R/q$. But R/q, and thus x, is rational, which is a contradiction. Therefore, our assumption is wrong and R must be irrational.

A similar indirect proof can be constructed to prove that the sum of a rational and an irrational number is itself irrational. Students often find it surprising that the sum and product of two irrational numbers is not necessarily irrational, as exemplified by the counterexamples in parts (*b*), (*e*), and (*g*) in task 5.3. Students should be asked to come up with other counterexamples to further demonstrate their understanding of these concepts. A final point that teachers might consider discussing through this task is exemplified in part (*e*): $\sqrt{3} \cdot \sqrt{3}$. Teachers may wish to rewrite this part using rational exponents, as $3^{1/2} \cdot 3^{1/2}$. The interesting case of using a rational exponent to represent an irrational number should be discussed with students, who might find this counterintuitive.

STANDARDS *for Mathematical Practice—Tasks 5.1 through 5.3*

Students develop mathematically proficient practices by solving the problems in the above tasks. By looking for patterns and examining related problems, students are extending their knowledge to make sense out of an unfamiliar concept. Students are also using the notions of proof by contradiction, and disproving statements by providing counterexamples. The three tasks presented in this section also support the Standards for Mathematical Practice listed on page vi, in particular standards 3 and 7.

MP.3

Task 5.2 requires that students address the reasoning of fictional students Susie and Matt. Students must "critique the reasoning" of these students, presenting arguments for why they do or do not agree with the statements made in task 5.2. Task 5.3, which builds upon the ideas presented in task 5.2, requires students to "recognize and use counterexamples" in order to disprove statements about the sums and products of irrational numbers (CCSSI 2010, p. 6). Further, in task 5.3, they must examine the various cases of sums and products, such as the sum of rational numbers, and the sum of a rational number and an irrational number, and so on, as exemplified in part II.

MP.7

In all three of the tasks presented above, students are required to examine the structure of mathematics. For task 5.1, students need to examine their prior knowledge about integral exponents, and they must extend that knowledge to rational exponents using what they know about the laws of exponents. By comparing the results of multiplying expressions with integral exponents—in parts (*a*), (*b*), and (*c*) of task 5.1—to the results of multiplying expressions with fractional exponents—in parts (*d*), (*e*), and (*f*) of task 5.1—

students conclude that $x^{1/2}$ must be equal to the square root of x, based on examining the mathematical structure of what they already know. Tasks 5.2 and 5.3 provide students with the opportunity to consider the structure of rational and irrational numbers, allowing them to draw conclusions about when sums and products of various pairs of rational and irrational numbers are themselves rational or irrational.

Quantities

To address the CCSS high school domain for N-Q, Quantities, real-life problems that require close attention to units are presented. Several problems in different chapters throughout this book also address this domain including, but not limited to, task 4.1 in Statistics and Probability, and tasks 2.5, 2.7, 2.10, and 2.11 in Functions.

Task 5.4 is an application of rational exponents, as developed above, by using the formula that relates the radius of a sphere to its volume. Teachers might want to consider presenting task 5.4 before the tasks in section 5.1 in order to motivate students to learn more about the topic. Discussion can ensue about what is "unusual" about the formula, leading students to want to learn how to work with the fractional exponent presented in the formula. Task 5.1 gives students the opportunity to discover the meaning of fractional exponents, which also enables them to complete task 5.4 successfully. In addition to addressing the standards in domain N-RN, "Extend the properties of exponents to rational exponents" (CCSSI 2010, p. 60), several standards in the functions domain F-IF are also addressed, mainly in the cluster "Interpret functions that arise in applications in terms of the context" (CCSSI 2010, p. 69).

Task 5.4

The formula that relates the radius of a sphere to its volume is $r = \left(\dfrac{3V}{4\pi}\right)^{\frac{1}{3}}$ where V is the volume and r is the radius.

(a) If the volume of a sphere is 1,000 cubic inches, what is the radius of the sphere in inches? In feet?

(b) If the radius of a sphere is 7 inches, what is the volume of the sphere in cubic inches? In cubic feet?

Task 5.4 has the dual purpose of providing an application of rational exponents, while requiring that students be mindful of the units of the problem. While in part (a) students only have to divide their answer in inches by 12 to convert to feet, part (b) requires a bit more thinking. The approximate volume of the sphere is 1436.8 in^3. This value must be divided by 12^3 in order to convert to cubic feet. Therefore, the approximate volume of the sphere in cubic feet is 0.83 ft^3. Further, if teachers so wished, they could develop the

"function" aspect of the problem, asking students to graph by hand or to use a graphing calculator or other utility. Volume would be the independent variable, while radius would be the dependent variable.

If teachers wished to do so, they could incorporate a more conceptual approach by beginning with the formula for the volume of a sphere as a function of its radius, which is $V = \frac{4\pi r^3}{3}$, and finding the inverse of this function on an appropriate domain. Students would then see that the fractional exponent ⅓ arises naturally from finding the inverse of a function that has an exponent of 3. This approach would involve Functions standard F-BF.4, "Find inverse functions," which is not necessarily intended for all students (CCSSI 2010, p. 70). Further, students could test by composition whether or not the functions are in fact inverses of each other.

Many other fascinating examples of real-life applications of fractional exponents can be found. One such example, which is quite remarkable, is the result that the square of the period of a planet is proportional to the cube of the average distance the planet is from the sun. That is, $T = D^{3/2}$, which is one of Kepler's laws. There are also examples from physics, astronomy, and many other content areas that students might find interesting (Sultan and Artzt 2010).

Task 5.5 provides an opportunity for students to compare different speeds by using "unit analysis" in order to convert between equal representations of units. The idea behind unit analysis is that any quantity may be multiplied by 1. For example, we can multiply by the fraction 1 minute/60 seconds (which equals 1) without changing the value of the original quantity.

Task 5.5

Sean plays baseball in Brooklyn, New York. His cousin Patrick plays soccer in Scotland. Sean's coach says that the speed of his pitches is about 50 miles per hour. Patrick's coach says that the speed of his kicks is about 20 meters per second. How can the boys compare their respective speeds? Who is faster in his sport?

The most important observation that students should make is that the quantities cannot be compared in their given form because they are expressed using different units of measure. Students should realize that there are two approaches to converting to the same units. They can either convert 50 miles per hour to meters per second, or they can convert 20 meters per second to miles per hour. They do not need to do both in order to answer the question. Teachers may, however, elect to have students solve the problem both ways in order to give them more opportunity for practice in conversion.

To convert 50 miles per hour to meters per second, students need to know that there are 60 seconds in one minute, 60 minutes in one hour, and that there are 1609.3 meters in a mile. The unit analysis is based on the variety of ways "one" can be expressed. For example, multiplying by the fraction $\frac{1 \text{ hour}}{60 \text{ min}}$ does not change a quantity because it is equal to 1. The following "string" of fractions would allow conversion from 50 miles per hour to meters per second:

$$\frac{50 \text{ miles}}{1 \text{ hour}} \cdot \frac{1 \text{ hour}}{60 \text{ min}} \cdot \frac{1 \text{ min}}{60 \text{ sec}} \cdot \frac{1609.3 \text{ meters}}{1 \text{ mile}}$$

Students are often confused by the logic used to determine this type of expression. Informally, they might be encouraged to think about creating fractions that allow them to "match up" units in the denominator with units in the numerator (and vice versa), thus enabling them to convert to the units they need. Therefore, since "hours" are in the denominator of the original fraction, we need to "match" hours in the numerator of a unit fraction, continuing until all the units are accounted for. In order to see the sequencing of why the above expression can be simplified, consider the following series of expressions. The first expression below simply separates the quantities from the units; for example, 50 miles is changed to 50 • 1 mile:

$$\frac{50 \cdot 1 \text{ mile}}{1 \text{ hour}} \cdot \frac{1 \text{ hour}}{60 \cdot 1 \text{ min}} \cdot \frac{1 \text{ min}}{60 \cdot 1 \text{ sec}} \cdot \frac{1609.3 \cdot 1 \text{ meter}}{1 \text{ mile}}$$

Next, using principles of multiplication of fractions, the entire expression can be rewritten as one fraction:

$$\frac{50 \cdot 1 \text{ mile} \cdot 1 \text{ hour} \cdot 1 \text{ min} \cdot 1609.3 \cdot 1 \text{ meter}}{1 \text{ hour} \cdot 60 \cdot 1 \text{ min} \cdot 60 \cdot 1 \text{ sec} \cdot 1 \text{ mile}}$$

We can then group the quantities in the beginning of the fraction so that the units are all together:

$$\frac{50 \cdot 1609.3 \cdot 1 \text{ mile} \cdot 1 \text{ hour} \cdot 1 \text{ min} \cdot 1 \text{ meter}}{60 \cdot 60 \cdot 1 \text{ mile} \cdot 1 \text{ hour} \cdot 1 \text{ min} \cdot 1 \text{ sec}}$$

Finally, we can rewrite as separate fractions:

$$\frac{50 \cdot 1609.3}{60 \cdot 60} \cdot \frac{1 \text{ mile}}{1 \text{ mile}} \cdot \frac{1 \text{ hour}}{1 \text{ hour}} \cdot \frac{1 \text{ min}}{1 \text{ min}} \cdot \frac{1 \text{ meter}}{1 \text{ sec}}$$

It is evident that several of the above fractions are equal to one; thus, we can rewrite as:

$$\frac{50 \cdot 1609.3}{60 \cdot 60} \cdot \frac{1 \text{ meter}}{1 \text{ sec}}$$

When simplified, this equals 22.4 meters per second. Students might find it helpful to see the above progression, even though it is unnecessary to carry out all these steps for every problem.

Similarly, if we wished to convert 20 meters per second to miles per hour we would use the following string and simplify in a similar way:

$$\frac{20\ \text{meters}}{1\ \text{sec}} \cdot \frac{60\ \text{sec}}{1\ \text{min}} \cdot \frac{60\ \text{min}}{1\ \text{hour}} \cdot \frac{1\ \text{mile}}{1609.3\ \text{meters}}$$

When simplified, we see that 20 meters per second is equal to 44.7 miles per hour. Either way, we can see that the speed of Sean's pitches is a bit faster than the speed of Patrick's soccer kicks.

STANDARDS *for Mathematical Practice—Tasks 5.4 and 5.5*

Students achieve the Standards for Mathematical Practice through problem solving in the above two tasks by relating an unfamiliar problem to a familiar one. They might also take a guess and check their result when solving the problems in this section. These tasks also support two of the Standards for Mathematical Practice (i.e., standards 4 and 6).

MP.4

The problem in task 5.4 allows students to model a real-life scenario using rational exponents, thus "apply[ing] the mathematics they know to solve problems arising in everyday life" (CCSSI 2010, p. 7). Students must be aware of how to convert between linear and cubic units, being careful to realize that there are 12^3 cubic inches in a cubic foot. Similarly, the conversion of units necessary to solve the problem in task 5.5 is a common technique used in many applications. Students must think carefully about the units and the conversions that they use, thus "identify[ing] important quantities in a practical situation" and "analyz[ing] . . . relationships mathematically to draw conclusions" (CCSSI 2010, p. 7).

MP.6

By carefully setting up and computing the "string" of units in order to make the appropriate conversion in task 5.5, students are "attend[ing] to precision" (CCSSI 2010, p. 7). Students must carefully set up the various units required to make the necessary conversion in terms of both units of time and units of distance. They must set up the units of conversion with the proper units in the numerator and in the denominator to allow for the unnecessary units to divide to 1.

The Complex Number System

Task 5.6 is designed to address the standards in the domain for the Complex Number System, specifically those in the cluster "Perform arithmetic operations with complex numbers," N-CN.1 and N-CN.2 (CCSSI 2010, p. 60). This task gives students what seems to be a deceptively simple problem that has no real solution, thus demonstrating the need for the existence of imaginary numbers.

Task 5.6

Find two numbers whose sum is 4 and whose product is 5.

Students might try in vain to find two such numbers that meet these conditions. Afterwards, they might attempt to represent the problem algebraically. The algebraic representation of this situation leads to the system of equations $x + y = 4$ and $xy = 5$. The first equation yields $y = 4 - x$, and when this is substituted into the second equation we get $5 = x(4 - x)$, or $4x - x^2 = 5$. One equivalent form of this is $x^2 - 4x + 5 = 0$. Students can now solve this using the quadratic formula. Their solution will look strange, since they will get $x = \frac{4 \pm \sqrt{-4}}{2}$, with a negative inside the radical.

Students might wonder what they should do with the -4 inside the radical, or what $\sqrt{-4}$ means, and if it is true that there is such a number such that $\sqrt{-4} \cdot \sqrt{-4}$ is equal to -4. After some discussion, students may be told that scientists and mathematicians have found it useful to treat square roots of negative numbers as if they were actual numbers and to define $\sqrt{-N}$ as $\sqrt{-N}$ times $\sqrt{-1}$ and refer to $\sqrt{-1}$ as i, which is called an "imaginary" number.

Students should be aware that $\sqrt{-2}$ times $\sqrt{-2}$ is not $\sqrt{(-2) \cdot (-2)}$ so that the multiplication rule that root(a) times root(b) equals root ab does not hold for negative numbers. To multiply them, we need to put them in i form. So $\sqrt{-4} = 2i$ and $2i$ times $2i = 4i^2 = -4$, as we wanted it to be.

In fact, scientists have found it useful to talk about complex numbers of the form $a + bi$, where a and b are real numbers. Electrical engineers use these numbers on a daily basis in the study of circuits, which is quite amazing considering that complex numbers simply result from defining the square root of -1 as i.

Task 5.7 is intended as an extension of task 5.6, so that students calculate the imaginary roots of the quadratic equation that they found, $x^2 - 4x + 5 = 0$. Then students are asked to relate their solutions to the original verbal problem in task 5.6, which was to find two numbers whose sum is 4 and whose product is 5.

Task 5.7

(a) Express the solutions to the quadratic equation you found in task 5.6 in imaginary form.

(b) Task 5.6 asked you to find two numbers whose sum is 4 and whose product is 5. Do these numbers satisfy these requirements? Why or why not?

By reinforcing to students that $i = \sqrt{-1}$ and that $\sqrt{-4}$ equals $\sqrt{-1} \cdot \sqrt{4}$, students should be able to express the solutions as $2 + i$ and $2 - i$. Part (*b*) asks students to consider what the sum and product of $2 + i$ and $2 - i$ might be. Students might be encouraged to make conjectures about what they think the sum and products of $a + bi$ and $c + di$ would be, and how $2 + i$ and $2 - i$ could have a sum of 4 and a product of 5. Teachers could then elicit from students that complex numbers are multiplied by using the distributive property of multiplication over addition, and they are added by combining like terms, remembering that $i^2 = -1$. One can pose the question of whether or not we can use the quadratic formula to solve all quadratic equations, and if the imaginary answers we get will always satisfy the equation. The answer is "yes," which students can see by solving several quadratic equations with imaginary roots (preferably with roots whose real and imaginary parts are whole numbers) and checking that the answers calculated through the use of the formula do in fact satisfy the equation. Students will get practice in working with imaginary numbers and will very likely be convinced that the definitions for addition and multiplication of complex numbers make sense and give meaningful answers.

STANDARDS *for Mathematical Practice—Tasks 5.6 and 5.7*

In this section, taking a conceptual approach to introducing imaginary numbers contributes to students' becoming mathematically proficient through problem solving by making sense of the unfamiliar result to what, at first glance, seems like a familiar problem. New knowledge is introduced and developed through the successful completion of the problem. Students may be able to achieve three Standards for Mathematical Practice by solving the problems in this section (i.e., standards 1, 2, and 7).

MP.1

Tasks 5.6 and 5.7 require that students make sense out of the results of what initially seems to be a somewhat simple problem—that is, finding two numbers that multiply to 5 and add to 4. When students use the quadratic formula and obtain a negative inside the radical, they are required to make some sense of what this might mean. After a discussion of mathematicians' decision to define $\sqrt{-1}$ to be i, task 5.7 asks students to make sense out of the complex numbers that they calculated in the context of the original problem. In determining whether it makes sense that $2 + i$ and $2 - i$ add to 4 and multiply to 5, students begin to make sense out of what it means to add and multiply complex numbers in general. Students must continually determine whether the unfamiliar values they have calculated make sense in the context of the problem and in the context of the new definition of the imaginary unit i, thus making sense of the problem and persevering in solving it (CCSSI 2010, p. 6).

MP.2

In incorporating the "new" imaginary unit i into their knowledge base, students are "reason[ing] abstractly and quantitatively" (CCSSI 2010, p. 6). In making sense of the way imaginary and complex numbers are defined and operated upon, students must "make sense of quantities and their relationships" (CCSSI 2010, p. 6). Students must attend "to the meaning of quantities" in order to make sense of how to compute using the new complex representations (CCSSI 2010, p. 6).

MP.7

Although students are initially unfamiliar with imaginary units and complex numbers, their knowledge of the real numbers and their operations allows insight into the operations of complex numbers, thus "look[ing] for and mak[ing] use of structure" (CCSSI 2010, p. 8). Even though the product of $2 + i$ and $2 - i$ is initially unknown, students can rely on the complex numbers' "inheriting" the right to use the distributive property of multiplication over addition in order to define the product. Similarly, students use the structure of real numbers to determine that $-i + i$ has a sum of zero, thus allowing a reasonable definition of the sum of $2 + i$ and $2 - i$.

Appendix

CCSS Overview for Middle and High School Mathematics

Grade 6						
Ratio and Proportion	The Number System/Number and Quantity	Expressions and Equations/Algebra	Geometry	Statistics and Probability	Functions	Modeling
• Understand ratio concepts and use ratio reasoning to solve problems.	• Apply and extend previous understandings of multiplication and division to divide fractions by fractions.	• Apply and extend previous understandings of arithmetic to algebraic expressions.	• Solve real-world and mathematical problems involving area, surface area, and volume.	• Develop understanding of statistical variability.		
	• Compute fluently with multi-digit numbers and find common factors and multiples.	• Reason about and solve one-variable equations and inequalities.		• Summarize and describe distributions.		
	• Apply and extend previous understandings of numbers to the system of rational numbers.	• Represent and analyze quantitative relationships between dependent and independent variables.				

	Grade 7				
Ratio and Proportion	**The Number System/Number and Quantity**	**Expressions and Equations/Algebra**	**Geometry**	**Statistics and Probability**	**Modeling**
• Analyze proportional relationships and use them to solve real-world and mathematical problems.	• Apply and extend previous understandings of operations with fractions to add, subtract, multiply, and divide rational numbers.	• Use properties of operations to generate equivalent expressions.	• Draw, construct, and describe geometrical figures and describe the relationships between them.	• Use random sampling to draw inferences about a population.	
		• Solve real-life and mathematical problems using numerical and algebraic expressions and equations.	• Solve real-life and mathematical problems involving angle measure, area, surface area, and volume.	• Draw informal comparative inferences about two populations.	
				• Investigate chance processes and develop, use, and evaluate probability models.	

Grade 8

Ratio and Proportion	The Number System/Number and Quantity	Expressions and Equations/Algebra	Geometry	Statistics and Probability	Functions	Modeling
	• Know that there are numbers that are not rational, and approximate them by rational numbers.	• Work with radicals and integer exponents.	• Understand congruence and similarity using physical models, transparencies, or geometry software.	• Investigate patterns of association in bivariate data.	• Define, evaluate, and compare functions.	
		• Understand the connections between proportional relationships, lines, and linear equations.	• Understand and apply the Pythagorean theorem.		• Use functions to model relationships between quantities.	
		• Analyze and solve linear equations and pairs of simultaneous linear equations.	• Solve real-world and mathematical problems involving volume of cylinders, cones, and spheres.			

			High School			
Ratio and Proportion	**The Number System/Number and Quantity**	**Expressions and Equations/Algebra**	**Geometry**	**Statistics and Probability**	**Functions**	**Modeling**
	• Extend the properties of exponents to rational exponents.	• Interpret the structure of expressions.	• Experiment with transformations in the plane.	• Summarize, represent, and interpret data on a single count or measurement variable.	• Understand the concept of a function and use function notation.	• Model real-world situations across curriculum.
	• Use properties of rational and irrational numbers.	• Write expressions in equivalent forms to solve problems.	• Understand congruence in terms of rigid motions.	• Summarize, represent, and interpret data on two categorical and quantitative variables.	• Interpret functions that arise in applications in terms of the context.	
	• Reason quantitatively and use units to solve problems.	• Perform arithmetic operations on polynomials.	• Prove geometric theorems.	• Interpret linear models.	• Analyze functions using different representations.	
	• Perform arithmetic operations with complex numbers.	• Understand the relationship between zeros and factors of polynomials.	• Make geometric constructions.	• Understand and evaluate random processes underlying statistical experiments.	• Build a function that models a relationship between two quantities.	
	• Represent complex numbers and their operations on the complex plane.	• Use polynomial identities to solve problems.	• Understand similarity in terms of similarity transformations.	• Make inferences and justify conclusions from sample surveys, experiments, and observational studies.	• Build new functions from existing functions.	

References

Common Core State Standards Initiative (CCSSI). *Common Core State Standards for Mathematics.* Washington, D.C.: National Governors Association Center for Best Practices and the Council of Chief State School Officers, 2010. http://www.corestandards.org.

Curcio, Frances R., and Sydney L. Schwartz. "What Does Algebraic Thinking Look Like and Sound Like with Preprimary Children?" *Teaching Children Mathematics* 3 (February 1997): 296–300.

Henderson, Kenneth B., and Robert E. Pingry. "Problem-Solving in Mathematics." In *The Learning of Mathematics: Its Theory and Practice,* edited by Howard F. Fehr, pp. 228–70. Washington, D.C.: National Council of Teachers of Mathematics, 1953.

Jones, Dustin L. "The Birthday Problem, Empirically." *Mathematics Teacher* 106, no. 6 (February 2012): 480.

Kline, Morris. *Mathematical Thought from Ancient to Modern Times.* New York: Oxford University Press, 1972.

Lesh, Richard, and Judith Zawojewski. "Problem Solving and Modeling." In *Second Handbook of Research on Mathematics Teaching and Learning,* edited by Frank K. Lester, Jr., pp. 763–804. Charlotte, N.C.: Information Age Publishing, and Reston, Va.: National Council of Teachers of Mathematics, 2007.

Lester, Jr., Frank K., and Paul E. Kehle. "From Problem Solving to Modeling: The Evolution of Thinking about Research on Complex Mathematical Activity." In *Beyond Constructivism,* edited by Richard Lesh and Helen M. Doerr, pp. 501–17. Mahwah, N.J.: Lawrence Erlbaum Associates, 2003.

National Council of Teachers of Mathematics (NCTM). *An Agenda for Action.* Reston, Va.: NCTM, 1980.

———. *Curriculum and Evaluation Standards for School Mathematics.* Reston, Va.: NCTM, 1989.

———. *Principles and Standards for School Mathematics.* Reston, Va.: NCTM, 2000.

———. *Algebra and Algebraic Thinking in School Mathematics.* 2008 Yearbook of the National Council of Teachers of Mathematics, edited by Carole E. Greenes. Reston, Va.: NCTM, 2008.

———. *Making It Happen: A Guide to Interpreting and Implementing* Common Core State Standards for Mathematics. Reston, Va.: NCTM, 2011.

O'Daffer, Phares, ed. *Problem Solving: Tips for Teachers.* Reston, Va.: NCTM, 1988.

Paulos, John Allen. *Innumeracy: Mathematical Illiteracy and Its Consequences.* New York: Hill and Wang, 1988.

Pickover, Clifford A. *The Math Book: From Pythagoras to the 57th Dimension, 250 Milestones in the History of Mathematics.* New York: Sterling, 2009.

Pollak, Henry O. "Introduction: What Is Mathematical Modeling?" In *Mathematical Modeling Handbook,* edited by Heather Gould, Diane R. Murray, and Andrew Sanfratello, pp. viii–xi. Bedford, Mass.: COMAP, 2011.

Pólya, George. *How to Solve It: A New Aspect of Mathematical Method.* 2nd ed. Princeton, N.J.: Princeton University Press, 1957.

Schaaf, William. "Mathematics and World History." *Mathematics Teacher* 23, no. 8 (December 1930): 496–503.

Schoenfeld, Alan H. "Problem Solving in the United States, 1970–2008: Research and Theory, Practice and Politics." *ZDM Mathematics Education* 39 (2007): 537–51.

Sultan, Alan, and Alice F. Artzt. *The Mathematics That Every Secondary School Math Teacher Needs to Know.* New York: Routledge, 2010.

von Mises, Richard. "Über Aufteilungs—und Besetzungs—Wahrsheinlichketien." *Revue de la Faculté des Sciences de l'Université d'Istanbul*, N.S. 4, 1939, pp. 145–63. Reprinted in *Selected Papers of Richard von Mises*, vol. 2, edited by Philipp Frank, Sydney Goldstein, Mark Kac, William Prager, Gábor Szegö, and Garrett Birkhoff, pp. 313–34. Providence, R.I.: American Mathematical Society, 1964.